Parental Advisory Manual

www.**rbooks**.co.uk

Natasha Desborough was born on the summer solstice in Wimbledon in 1974, which makes her part hippy and part Womble. She grew up in Croydon, the armpit of south London, and went to a posh all-girls school before discovering the joys of booze, fags and boys at sixth-form college in Reigate.

Natasha started her career as a runner on feature films and pop videos, but soon realized that was shit and left to help set up and run a radio station for her favoured football club, Crystal Palace. Her time was mainly spent watching Palace lose dreadfully and snogging lots of footballers. After that came *The Chill Out Room* on XFM, a great big, throbbing, pervy show, full of erotic poetry and sexy music. It was filthy dirty but she needed the money. Then it was on to the XFM *Breakfast Session* for a year before finding happiness on the mid-morning show.

Natasha joined BBC 6 Music to host the *Weekend Breakfast Show* in 2005, became a TV entertainment pundit, had a couple of kids and lost her social life. She lives in Croydon with her partner Jim and young sons Oscar and Wilfie.

www.natashadesborough.co.uk
www.parentaladvisorymanual.co.uk

Parental Advisory Manual

Natasha Desborough

BANTAM PRESS

LONDON • TORONTO • SYDNEY • AUCKLAND • JOHANNESBURG

TRANSWORLD PUBLISHERS
61–63 Uxbridge Road, London W5 5SA
A Random House Group Company
www.rbooks.co.uk

First published in Great Britain
in 2009 by Bantam Press
an imprint of Transworld Publishers

This book is a work of non-fiction based on the life, experiences and recollections of the author.
In some cases names of people, sequences or the detail of events have been changed solely to
protect the privacy of others. The author has stated to the publishers that, except in such minor
respects not affecting the substantial accuracy of the work, the contents of this book are true.

A CIP catalogue record for this book
is available from the British Library.

ISBN 9780593064184

Addresses for Random House Group Ltd companies outside the UK
can be found at: www.randomhouse.co.uk
The Random House Group Ltd Reg. No. 954009

The Random House Group Limited supports The Forest Stewardship
Council (FSC), the leading international forest-certification organization. All our
titles that are printed on Greenpeace-approved FSC-certified paper carry the FSC logo.
Our paper procurement policy can be found at
www.rbooks.co.uk/environment

Typeset in 10/15pt Helvetica Neue by
Falcon Oast Graphic Arts Ltd
Printed and bound in Great Britain by
Clays Ltd, Bungay, Suffolk

2 4 6 8 10 9 7 5 3 1

Mixed Sources
Product group from well-managed
forests and other controlled sources
www.fsc.org   Cert no. TT-COC-2139
© 1996 Forest Stewardship Council

For Oscar, Wilfie and Jim

Contents

Acknowledgements

So here comes the gushing bit:

Huge thanks to Susan Smith, Sarah Emsley, Lucy Sweet and Kate Samano for making my dream become a reality. I am now officially 'an author'. Hooray!

To Mum for giving me a wonderful childhood and for not disowning me after reading this book (I hope), and to Dad for always seeing the funny side. Also, to my brother Alex for designing the fabulous website that created such a buzz about the book.

A special thank you to my boys, Oscar and Wilfie, for the love, laughter and joy that you have brought to my world, and to Jim for being a fabulous father and my best friend.

On behalf of all mummies and daddies, thank you to all the CBeebies presenters and actors for allowing us to have secret rude thoughts about you.

To Vikki Rimmer for your support, kindness and for giving me the confidence to write this book in the first place. To Deana Murfitt for being inspirational and for making me laugh.

And of course the biggest thanks go to all the brilliant parents and individuals who have showed support or contributed to this book (or both!). Some entries didn't make it into the final edit but every single story submitted was greatly appreciated. Your humour has made this book a pleasure to write. Whilst there are too many people to name in this small space, I would especially like to acknowledge Solance Scholey, Verity Maidlow, Catherine Bittles, Freddie Eden, Angela Ferrara, Emma Harvey, Claire McCall, Nancy Oliver, Zoë and Nick Bonell and Lisa Carruthers. Thank you. You are all stars! xxx

INTRODUCTION

Let's be honest, when seemingly smug mums and dads tell you that parenthood changes your life, they're not joking. Kids turn your world upside-down and then flip it round and round until you don't know whether to scratch your baby or burp your bum.

Parenthood transforms so much about your everyday existence. It makes you say things you would never usually say, like fufflenuff or blurglegunt (see chapter fifteen), and leads you to wonder if Father Christmas is actually nothing more than a filthy nonce (see chapter twelve). It can manipulate mummies into naming their lady garden 'Lulu' (see chapter eight) and can cause daddies to have sex fantasies about Miss Hoolie from *Balamory* (see chapter eleven). It can make you dress your child like the Fonz (see chapter fourteen) and may cause you to

11

believe that Jolene moustache bleach should be available free on the NHS (see chapter thirteen).

These are important and overlooked issues of parenthood that so-called parenting gurus tend to ignore. I believe these issues should be forgotten no longer, so I've written this book for parents like me, who love their kids more than anything else in the world but will hold up their hands and admit that being a mum or dad isn't the perpetually blissful and rewarding experience that we had been led to believe. Mummies and daddies – welcome to the *Parental Advisory Manual*.

1. PARENTAL EXPECTATIONS

Birth Plan

We expect so much when we decide to have kids. Like most first-time mothers, I attended antenatal classes and planned the birth of my baby down to the finest detail, believing that I would be fully in control for the duration. I wrote a detailed birth plan to give to the midwife: 'no student doctors fiddling with my fanny, thank you very much', I was having a natural water birth with the sweet reassuring scent of Neroli wafting from a burner, and I would require absolutely no pain relief because the elation of childbirth would make me feel empowered and would drive me on to the end. (Crikey, those pregnancy hormones are as powerful as class-A drugs). My baby was going to make a natural, wonderful, gentle entrance into the world because I'd planned it meticulously.

Then reality came crashing down around me with full force. My birth plan never even came out of my overnight bag. In the end I endured a slow, thirty-six-hour labour, and after much prodding and undignified poking (by consultants *and* bloody student doctors), it was decided that the only option was for me to have an emergency Caesarean.

I can recall being absolutely terrified at the prospect of a major operation and was convinced that my baby would die. Yet at the same time, I was getting all worked up about having my pubes shaved off and was complaining furiously to a nurse about the gaping hole at the back of my hospital gown. The operation itself was quick and efficient, and I remember a lovely sweet nurse listening patiently as I demanded to know why the only male member of staff in the operating theatre had the job of putting a suppository up my bum. Why hadn't I been warned about this in my NCT class?

Things Real Parents Weren't Told in Antenatal Class but Wish They Had Been

Babies don't sleep like babies.

'What stupid fool came up with the phrase "to sleep like a baby"? Babies don't bloody sleep. And if they do sleep then it's for such a short amount of time that it doesn't actually count as sleep. Whenever I hear someone using that nonsensical phrase I want to go over and slap them.'

Some women 'really' enjoy childbirth.

'I read an article in a magazine all about women who achieve orgasm during childbirth. I wish they'd told me that in antenatal classes as I'd have packed my vibrator in my overnight bag.'

You just won't care.

'I was so worried about pooing myself during childbirth that I didn't care about anything else. Never mind the pain, the stitches, the dangers or the blood and gore. I was just terrified that I'd do a big number two in front of everyone and I was very concerned that it might land on my baby's head as he came out. I thought it would be such an awful way to come into the world. I needn't have worried. When I was pushing that baby out it could have been raining shit in the delivery room for all I cared.'

 ### Your midwife is a gamble.
'Unless you are lucky enough to have the same midwife throughout your pregnancy, the personality of the midwife you actually get on the day is a lottery. My midwife was worryingly eccentric. She was into New Age stuff and wanted me to rub a crystal on my tummy each time I had a contraction. She said it would help the baby tune in to my vibes. The gas and air wasn't doing anything for me, so I was up for trying anything to help ease the pain. I rubbed the crystal all over my tummy as I was doubled up in agony but it did absolutely sod all.'

Gas and air is bad for daddies.

'During the final stage of labour I was getting on my wife's nerves and I don't think she really cared if I was there or not. I was getting stressed as she was in so much pain and I couldn't do anything to help, so I thought I would try some gas and air to see if it relaxed me. I had a few big tokes and the room started spinning. Next thing I remember, my face was in a pool of vomit and the midwife was kicking me in the head and saying, "Mr Smith, you have a healthy baby boy." I first held my son with my own sick on my face. It wasn't what we had planned.'

2. HOLY PARENTING

The Sermon

Before I had children of my own, I knew that I would be the best parent in the world. My baby would wear eco-friendly nappies so I would not be contributing to the enormous nappy mountains that engulf landfill sites. My toddler would not shriek annoyingly in restaurants and bother other people who were dining without children. My child would never have a full-on screaming temper tantrum by the checkout at Sainsbury's, and wouldn't dream of eating an entire copy of *The Very Hungry Caterpillar* at the local library. And my naked child would never wee all over the floor in the swimming-pool changing area in full view of everyone whilst singing 'I like to move it, move it'. But of course, that's exactly what happened.

Everyone starts out as a good parent. And then they have kids. Bookshop shelves are straining under the sheer weight of parenting books, all laying down the guidelines of child-rearing. But our babies and children don't necessarily stick to the rules and sometimes it's just too difficult to follow the blueprint. We do the best we possibly can as parents, but it's pretty much impossible to be perfect all of the time. Or even some of the time! We are constantly reminded of our parental failures, so who can we turn to in our moments of desperation? Well, don't look at me – I've got no idea what I'm doing when it comes to raising kids! I just make it up as I go along.

But in the absence of any kind of divine parental guidance, here are my Ten Commandments of parenting.

The Ten Commandments of Parenting

✱ *Thou shalt not attempt to achieve the post-baby figure of an A-list celebrity.* Remember, they are not normal. Try to think of them as like Dr Who – when their bodies become tired, saggy, withered and knackered, they are able to regenerate into a younger, more radiant form. Of course their special-effects team consists of a personal trainer, nanny, surgeon, hairdresser, stylist, make-up artist, masseur and dermatologist rather than just a couple of computer geeks knobbing about on a Mac, but the result is the same. A brand-new, better person. But just like Dr Who, post-baby A-list bodies are simply fantasy.

✱ **Thou shalt not be lazy about snot.**
Before I had children of my own I used to look with disgust at toddlers whose faces were caked in snot. And not just yucky fresh snot. I'm talking about old, yellowing, crusty snot too. Fresh snot and crusty snot at the same time. A facial snot-fest. 'Bad parent,' I would think. But now I understand. Now I too have used up an entire roll of toilet paper in just one morning wiping the endless rivers of snot that flow from a child's nose to his mouth. As fast as I wipe it off, it just keeps reappearing, cascading like a nasal waterfall. And it goes on for days and weeks. And then, just when you think the snot flow has stopped, it all starts again. Your wastepaper

bins, handbag and pockets are overflowing with snot rags. You are no longer a person in your own right. You are nothing more than a common bogey-wiper. Eventually the mucus grinds you down and so you give up the wiping because there's no point. You have hit rock bottom and you just can't be bothered any more. Now do you understand?

* **Thou shalt not have it off with the gorgeous stay-at-home dad whose kids attend the same playgroup as yours.**
He may well understand how monotonous, lonely, stressful and difficult your days can be. He may well be able to sympathize in a way that you can only dream that your partner would. He may well look like David Beckham and be hilarious, kind, sensitive and great with kids, but he's not yours so do NOT touch.

* **Thou shalt not buy plastic toys.**
Wooden toys are attractive, durable and environmentally friendly. Plastic toys are

bad. They are made from non-renewable sources and are difficult to recycle. Wood or plastic? It's as fundamental as good versus evil. But given the choice between a classic wooden train set and an electric Thomas the Tank Engine plastic railway, your average toddler would pick Thomas every time. Just remember that the future of our planet is in their mucky little hands. Oh crikey.

✳ *Thou shalt not lie to your child.*
Except when it's absolutely necessary. For example, you are in a restaurant when your four-year-old daughter lifts her dress up to her chest and thrusts her finger deep into her belly button. You say, 'Please don't do that.'

She ignores you and continues to vigorously examine her navel. You try again a little louder.

'I said please don't do that.'

She ignores you.

'Emily, pull your dress back down and leave it alone.'

She ignores you.

'LEAVE. IT. ALONE.'

No response.

'Emily, if you don't stop fiddling with your belly button, your bottom will fall off.'

She looks up in horror and immediately takes her finger out of her navel and pulls her dress back down. Job done.

* **Thou shalt not sniff your child's nappy.**

You always said you wouldn't do it, but now it's as natural as breathing. You're chatting to a mummy at playgroup when you suddenly get a quick whiff of poo – just a fleeting hint on the breeze. Is it just a blow-off? Is the smell coming from your child or one of the other kids lurking near by? Only one way to find out. You scoop up your child and sniff his or her bottom. No one bats an eyelid. It's what parents do. But the old you would be repulsed. Remember that!

* **Thou shalt not use the TV as a babysitter.**

Yes, we all know that too much TV is bad for

our children, blah, blah, blah, so if you have ever sat your child down in front of *Charlie and Lola* just so that you could run the vacuum cleaner round the house or do the washing-up, then I'm calling Social Services.

✳ *Thou shalt not utter the words 'because I said so.'*

You would never, ever utter these words to your child, would you? Of course not, because you encourage communication at all times.

Conversation is an integral part of your child's upbringing. You are always happy to answer any question thrown at you. Any question at all. Any question except 'Why?' Three letters that will eventually make even the most saintly and patient parent lose the will to live.

'OK, can you get in the car, please?'
'Why?'
'Because we are going to see Matthew.'
'Why?'
'Because he's invited you round for lunch.'

'Why?'

'Because he would like to play with you.'

'Why?'

'Because he's your friend. Now hurry up and get in the car.'

'Why?'

'Just hurry up, please.'

'Why?'

'We're going to be late.'

'Why?'

'Because you won't hurry up.'

'Why?'

'Get in the car.'

'Why?'

'I. Said. Get. In. The. Car. NOW.'

'Why?'

'ARGGGGGGGH!!!! BECAUSE I SAID SO.'

* **Thou shalt not call your partner 'Mummy' or 'Daddy',**

especially when the kids aren't about. It's a bit creepy, makes everyone around you feel awkward and lets everybody know that your sex life is a thing of the past. Do you really want to be that transparent?

* *Thou shalt not be jealous of your friends with no children.*
Thou shalt not envy their ability to be spontaneous and have a fun and fulfilling social life. Thou shalt not covet their spotless cream sofas, uncluttered rooms and toy-free floors. And thou shalt not crave their wild and exciting sex lives.

3. NAMES

The Name Game

Naming your child is a big deal and bloody difficult. Do you pick a name that's popular, so that your child will blend quietly into their social environment, or do you give him or her a name that will stand out from the others? Do you pick a name that declares, 'My parents are dull and boring,' or choose a name that shouts, 'My parents are pretentious arseholes'? You see, not only do you have to worry about the social label you are giving your child, but you also have to be aware that the name of your offspring reveals a whole lot about you as a parent.

For my oldest son Oscar's third birthday, I invited a few of his closest friends and their parents to a birthday picnic in the park. It was a beautiful summer's day and the park was full of children laughing and playing in the sun. From all around came the sound of mums and dads calling to their children: 'Ella . . . Joshua . . . Grace . . . Jack . . . Emily . . . Oliver . . . don't go too far.' Our gang of kids were running around all over the place and when lunch was laid out and ready, I decided to round them up so they could all sit down to eat.

'OSCAR, WILFRED, PHILOMENA, VERITY, PRENTICE, CASSIUS, ARTHUR . . . LUNCH IS READY.'

Christ on a bike. Where was I? Ponceville Park?

I hoped these names wouldn't see our children bullied and ridiculed at school to such an extent that they would go on to develop personal insecurities and social anxiety disorders that would mess up their adult lives, leading them to seek therapy and realize how irresponsible it was of their parents to give them such arty-farty names. Their only option would then be to pack up and emigrate to Australia to get as far away from their evil parents as possible. Oh my God. You can drive away your children by giving them pretentious names. That's another tick in the 'bad parenting' box then.

These days, of course, parents have become very aware of the social power of names, and none more so than celebrities. Innocent celebrity babies are born into the world with colourful and ridiculous name tags such as 'Muffi-Jo Tallulacrotch', which declare, 'I am a very special person and my parents are fabulously original and talented.'

In fact we *expect* celebrities to choose stupid names for their children. Let's face it, David and Victoria Beckham would be nowhere near as glamorous if their kids were called Barry, Rodney and Charlie instead of Brooklyn, Romeo and Cruz, would they? No way. Celebs need to differentiate between themselves and us mere mortals. Remember, the jazzier the name, the brighter the lights.

Although originality is the number-one factor for stars to consider when naming their offspring, it is possible to pigeonhole celebrity baby names into a small number of sub-categories.

Types of Celebrity Names

The 'Mini-Me' Name

★ To name a child after yourself is either a sign of pure laziness or sheer arrogance. Either way, Nigella Lawson must be pretty pissed off with her dad. I mean, come on, Nigel, what were you thinking?

★ Jermaine Jackson of the Jackson 5 actually has a child called Jermajesty. Jermaine took his ego to a whole new level, and then crowned it.

✷ Former heavyweight boxer George Foreman has ten (count 'em, ten!) children. He began the name game just fine with his daughters Natalie, Michi, Leona and Freeda. But then he went seriously off track. Maybe his success and fame went to his head. Perhaps he was punch drunk. Who the heck knows? But Georgemania definitely got the better of him. He named his first-born son George Junior, then his second son George III. Next up was George IV, then George V (can you see a pattern developing?) and George VI. Then, just when you thought George VII was set to become child number ten, along came Papa George's fifth daughter. Hurrah! The Georgemania cycle had been broken. So what beautiful name was given to the youngest member of the Foreman family? Georgetta. Nice one, Dad!

The 'Seemed Like a Good Idea at the Time (When I Was Off My Face)' Name

✴ David and Angie Bowie set the bar pretty high for embarrassing celebrity baby names when poor little Zowie Bowie was born in 1971. Yes, it may well be a terrible name, but at least it rhymes. It flows. Like Ziggy Stardust song lyrics. And thus David Bowie laid down the rhyming-name gauntlet. His best buddy Marc Bolan took up the challenge when his son was born a few years later, by naming him Rolan. Rolan Bolan. If only he could have found a Nolan sister to love him.

✴ Vanilla Ice's real name is Robert Van Winkle. Yes, it's a rubbish name, but is that any excuse to take out your resentment on your poor innocent kids? The little Winkles are called Dusti Rain and Keelee Breeze. Still I'm sure his eldest daughter is thankful that her dad opted for the alternative second name, as Dusti Winkle would have been horrendous.

The 'Fruity' Name

✳ When Bob Geldof and Paula Yates named their second daughter Peaches Honeyblossom we all thought it was pretty tame compared to their first daughter, whom they had named Fifi Trixibelle. I guess Peaches is supposed to be a kind of soft, sweet, pretty sort of name, but I just can't help thinking of arses whenever I see her mug on the TV. Great big, hairy, peachy buttocks. Do you see?

✳ The world is still unsure as to why Coldplay front man Chris Martin and actress Gwyneth Paltrow named their first child Apple. Yes, it's certainly different, but it's hardly the most exciting name in the world. Personally I think that Chris and Gwyneth really missed a trick with their daughter. Apple Martin is just one vowel away from being an Apple Martini. Now that would have been a *proper* showbiz name.

The 'Culture Vulture' Name

✳ The Culture Vulture name is used by a lot of

celebrities to show off their fabulous and hip taste in the arts. So glossy showbiz couple Gwen Stefani and Gavin Rossdale wasted no time in giving their second son an über-cool name. Ladies and gentlemen, may we introduce you to Zuma Nesta Rock. *Zuma* is the name of a critically acclaimed album by the Godfather of Grunge, Neil Young. Nesta was Bob Marley's first name before an immigration official switched it with his middle name, Robert. And, of course, Rock was probably chosen because Gavin and Gwen are rock stars. Aah, see, now it all makes perfect sense.

✷ Sean Penn and Robin Wright named their son Hopper, after the Hollywood actor Dennis Hopper and not, as I had first assumed, after the big orange seventies Space Hoppers. Although, to be honest, I don't know which is worse – to be named after a large, bottom-smacked rubber ball or a crazy, drug-addled 1960s rebel, who was recently seen in an American TV drama chatting happily to his own penis. You decide.

✳ Gary Oldman and Donya Fiorentino were obviously great fans of Jonathan Swift as they decided to name their son Gulliver Flynn. I'm guessing that Flynn may be a little nod to the great Errol Flynn, who apparently could tap out 'You Are My Sunshine' with his famously enormous winkie on a piano keyboard. Now that's talent.

The 'Just Because' Name

✳ American actress Shannyn Sossamon has a young son called Audio Science. Her explanation is that she simply chose words that were special to her. That's all very well, but those two words are also very special to the type of nerdy geeks who wear beige tank-tops and jumbo corduroys and never have girlfriends. Ten quid he changes his name to Bert Beefcake by the time he's nineteen.

✳ Tamika Scott from American R&B band Xscape gave her baby the funky name of O'shun. Not Ocean. O'shun. It's all about the spelling and that super-important apostrophe. This seems to be a bit of a trend in the States at the moment, as the rapper Ice Cube has named his child O'shea. Don't be surprised if some time in the near future *Hello!* magazine prints exclusive pictures of Eminem with his unplanned surprise son, named O'shit.

What's in a Name?

When my partner Jim and I finally agreed that our first son would be called Oscar, a number of factors had helped us make our decision. For starters, Oscar Wilde's *The Picture of Dorian Gray* is one of my favourite novels. We also thought it was a strong name, it went well with Jim's surname, we really liked it and it wasn't too popular. But one other thing really nailed it for us. When we told our parents, they all hated it. And there is nothing more satisfying than winding up your parents!

The reasons for choosing a baby's name can be really quite bizarre. Aside from simply following trends, cultural influences can often be a motive behind the parents' final decision.

Real Parents' Inspiration for Their Children's Names

Big Ben. 'Some people think it's a bit strange that I named my son after a massive clock in London. But he isn't actually named after the clock. He's named after the bell. It's well over a hundred years old and that makes it history. It annoys me that people get the clock and the bell confused. It's the bell that's called Big Ben, not the clock. So Ben is named after a bell. The end.' (_Insert your own 'bell-end' gag here!_)

_R.E.M._ 'I wanted to call my daughter Michael, after the singer Michael Stipe, but my wife wouldn't let me. She said that Michael was a boy's name and wouldn't accept that it could also be used as a girl's name. Stupid woman. So we settled for Rachel Emily Marston, so at least she has the initials R.E.M.' (_The daddy is right – the mum from_ The Waltons _was called Michael in real life, as was the bass player from_ The Bangles. _But it's still a bobbins name for a girl._)

♀ *Bella Emberg*. 'I'd always wanted to name my first-born daughter Bella, after Bella Emberg from *The Russ Abbot Show*. As a little boy I used to wish that she was my mum, especially when she was dressed as Blunder Woman. She was so funny. Is she still alive?' (*Yes, I know! This one is seriously weird.*)

♂ *George Michael*. 'My son George was named after George Michael, but I told my husband that I wanted to name him after George Clooney. I don't think he would have liked to name his son after a man who wanks off in public toilets.' (*When it's put like that, I think she's probably right.*)

♀ *Mother Teresa*. 'Our daughter was going to be named after Mother Teresa, an incredible humanitarian and an extraordinary woman. However, I was utterly shocked and appalled to discover that her full name, Teresa Berkeley, would have been the same as a famous nineteenth-century British dominatrix. To think that my innocent little girl might be associated with a filthy whore is almost as bad as if she actually turned to prostitution in later life. Isn't anything sacred any more?' (*Clearly a man with a few issues here!*)

👩 *Russell Brand.* 'My son Russell was named after the comedian Russell Brand. He's just so gorgeous – so sexy it's untrue. I love his hair and his bum and his long, sexy legs. I'm talking about Russell Brand, by the way. My son has nice hair and legs, but he's not sexy.' (*Pop trivia alert: Russell Brand loves The Smiths so much that he named his cat Morrissey.*)

👨 *Dr Who.* 'I chose our son's middle name, Gallifrey, which is the name of the planet where Dr Who comes from. My wife hates it, but she chose his first name, Arthur, which I hate. So it's actually worked out really well, because we're even in our hate for our son's names.' (*Grrreat! You can't beat parental harmony!*)

👩 *Pride and Prejudice.* 'I think it's pretty obvious where the inspiration for my daughter D'arcy's name came from! *Pride and Prejudice* is my favourite book of all time and I loved the BBC adaptation. Colin Firth as Mr Darcy coming back from a swim all wet and yummy – I just had to name my child after such a delicious character.' (*What is it with these parents who name their kids after people they fancy? It's Oedipal wrongness.*)

U2. 'I wanted my son's middle name to be Bono, but my wife wouldn't let me because she thinks Bono is a big tit.' (*And she's right.*)

Simon Cowell. 'Simon Cowell is the biggest star on TV at the moment. He's charismatic, funny, handsome and just oozes confidence. He's how I think a man should be, which is why I chose to name my son after him. My boyfriend wasn't too keen on the name Simon at first, as it rhymes with "hymen" and he didn't think that was very nice, but I won him over in the end.' (*I'm not sure what's more disturbing – associating all Simons with the membrane that partially covers a woman's vagina or naming your child after a man who looks like an Ewok with a flat-top.*)

4. BREAST-FEEDING

Express Yourself

So much has been written about breastfeeding: the benefits, the disadvantages, the stress, the pain, the pleasure, the guilt, the disapproval, the simplicity, etc, etc. But there are a few areas that haven't been covered by parenting manuals, and we're going to focus on those now.

I have experienced the pros and cons of both breastfeeding and bottle-feeding, and one aspect of breastfeeding that was consistent with both of my babies was my ability to express milk. At one point I had to get to grips with the hospital breast pump, which was more like a piece of industrial machinery than a gentle, breast-milk-extracting device. It was the loudest, most powerful pump in the world and stretched my nipples to the size of totem poles. I'm not joking. I could have picked gherkins out of a jar with them. They've never been the same since.

We all know what's going on when a baby is suckling on the breast, but to actually see the milk coming out of your breasts is quite weird and perhaps a little bit exciting (but *not* in a sex way). And it seems that I'm not the only person to get a bit of a thrill from expressing milk.

Real Parents' Top Five Revolting Expressed-Breast-Milk Stories

 'Like most dads, I was curious to find out what breast milk tasted like. My girlfriend thought I was disgusting and ordered me *never* to taste it, but one evening when she was asleep, I snuck a little sip from a bottle of expressed breast milk that she had left in the fridge. It was lovely. So lovely, in fact, that I developed a bit of a taste for it and would sneak little sips when the missus wasn't looking. I haven't had any breast milk for eighteen months now, since she has stopped breastfeeding, but I've been tempted to buy some off the internet. That's gross, isn't it? Sorry.' (*A secret breast-milk drinker? What would R Whites think?*)

 'One afternoon, after I'd been expressing milk, a couple of girlfriends dropped by to see my seven-week-old baby and have a chat. I was still quite doolally from lack of sleep, hormones and general mummy madness and wasn't firing on all cylinders. I made my friends a cup of tea, got the biscuits out and sat down for a good old gossip. As we were chatting, I noticed that the tea tasted a bit odd, but as my friends hadn't mentioned anything, I ignored it. It was only when I went back into the kitchen to turn the sterilizer on that I realized with horror that I had accidentally put breast milk into the cups of tea instead of regular milk. I didn't tell my friends, obviously, as I think they would probably have barfed there and then – I know I almost did.' (*It's kind of like a grown-up version of being 'blood sisters', isn't it? Aah! They are all bonded for life now.*)

'I produced ridiculous amounts of milk and there just wasn't enough room in the freezer for it all. So rather than waste it, I would often put it on the kid's cornflakes, and if I had any extra breast milk left over, I would give it to our cat, Foo Foo, who loved it and lapped up every last bit. I don't think it's gross – just economical.' (*The most disturbing part of this anecdote is that she calls her pussy Foo Foo.*)

'Last winter, my wife and I invited some friends over for the evening. I poured everyone a glass of Baileys before realizing that we didn't have any ice cubes in the freezer. But then I noticed the cubes of frozen breast milk that were sitting in a tray. So I popped them in the glasses and served them to our guests. Everyone commented on how fantastic the milk ice cubes tasted with the Baileys and all was going well until my wife suddenly twigged what I'd done. To say she went mental is an understatement! Of course she didn't do it in front of our friends, so they obliviously drank their Baileys and breast milk quite happily, but I was in big trouble when they had gone home.' (*Breast milk and Baileys cocktails. It could catch on.*)

 'I came up with a rather ingenious way to use up the copious amounts of expressed breast milk that I was producing for my four-month-old baby. I made breast-milk ice lollies, which my three-year-old son would happily eat in the summer time. Did I ever give one to any of my son's friends? Yes! A few times. They all loved them.' (*Yucky, yucky.*)

Shooting Guns

One of the most embarrassing things about breastfeeding is the accidental milk squirts that can happen without warning. Actually, the word 'squirt' doesn't really do the action justice. A lactating woman can shoot milk from her breast in a powerful stream that can land metres away. It's amazing. The best party trick *ever.*

One mummy recalled a time when she was dining with a friend in a pizzeria and breastfeeding her baby very discreetly: 'The gentleman who was sitting with his wife on the next table wouldn't stop giving me disapproving looks and kept tutting loudly every few minutes. He was really making me feel uncomfortable, so after about half an hour of him staring at me I finally snapped and said, "Look, I'm sorry if you don't approve, but I can assure you that if you stopped staring at my breasts, you wouldn't even notice there was a baby here at all." It was at that precise moment that my baby decided to pull away from my boob and an enormous jet of milk shot into the air and landed about half an inch away from the man's foot. I quickly tucked my exposed bosom away and said to the man, "And if you don't stop staring at me, next time I'll aim directly at your eyeball."'

It's like a super power, isn't it? Mega Mummy and her milk-squirting laser beams. Just one squirt can blind you instantly.

Real Mummies' Top Ten Accidental Squirting-Breast-Milk Targets

* Stranger's laptop on a train.
* Father-in-law's forehead.
* Back of a passenger's head on a bus.
* Husband's mouth.

* Stranger sitting three seats away in a cinema.
* Her dining partner's pizza.
* The inside of a Starbucks window.
* Hairdresser's eye.
* The tasselly leather jacket of a man waiting at a bus stop.
* Breastfeeding counsellor's lip.

Night Nursing

Feeding your baby in the early hours is supposed to be an intimate experience for you and your child. Whether you are breastfeeding or bottle-feeding in the still of the night, nothing could be more natural and satisfying. But when it's four o'clock in the morning and the third time you've had to get up, and your head hurts, your eyes are sore, you are tearful and exhausted to your very core and your other half is lying next to you snoring like a pig, doing the night feed can be a far from beautiful experience. So how do parents while away the hours when they are doing the night feeds?

Real Parents' Top Five Things to Do to Pass the Time During Night Feeds

 'I bottle-fed my baby, the idea being that my husband and I would share the night-feed duties. That was the idea, but no matter how hard I kicked my husband, I just couldn't get him to wake up to do his turn so it was always me who did the night feeds. So to pass the time, I used to try to remember the names of all the men I had snogged before I got married. I couldn't remember all of them but there were well over a hundred. I was a bit of a goer before I settled down. I was hot stuff. My husband should remember that. I was HOT!'

 'I've always had a passion for death-metal music but my wife will never let me play any in the house because she finds it too offensive. So whenever I had to get up to do the night feed, I would always take the baby downstairs and give him his milk whilst listening to my favourite band, Cannibal

Corpse. My son and I were so content together and I will always cherish those precious hours, with "Butchered At Birth" by Cannibal Corpse providing the soundtrack to beautiful father-and-son bonding moments.'

♀ 'I thought I was a bit of an earth mother and would breastfeed my newborn baby naked every two hours during the night. It was a lovely time when I felt so peaceful and close to him, but I got into a strange habit of reciting Philip Larkin's 'This Be the Verse' when he was on my breast. It's not really very maternal to be repeating "They fuck you up, your mum and dad" over and over again, is it?'

♂ 'My girlfriend and I would take it in turns to do the night feeds when my baby son was tiny. I would always insist on doing the eleven-thirty feed so that I could take my son downstairs, turn on the TV and watch the ten minutes of free porn that comes on every night, while giving him a bottle. What?! Look, it's the only bit of action I saw for about a year. Give me a break!'

 'I always found night feeds very boring, so I dug out a box from the attic that contained a load of old *Just Seventeen* magazines from the late eighties to amuse myself. I would sit and feed my baby and reread the teenage-angst-ridden problem pages and think to myself, "Ha! You think you're hard done by at fourteen with your fat corned-beef legs and no boyfriend – just wait till your tits become spaniel ears, your tummy looks like an empty haggis and your fanny is knackered. Then you'll know what it's like to feel hard done by."'

5. SLEEP DEPRIVATION

The Twilight Zone

Everyone knows that in the first few months after the birth of a baby, the parents become walking zombies through lack of sleep. What the parenting books fail to mention is that sleep deprivation can continue for years.

Alternative Controlled Crying

Some parents (and I include myself) swear by 'controlled crying'. For those not in the know, controlled crying is a sleep-training technique whereby you leave your baby to cry for progressively longer periods of time until he or she settles. I'm not going to lie to you – it's bloody hard work – but if you are about to have a total meltdown, controlled crying can be a very effective method. Here's how to get the best results.

✱ **STEP 1** Put your baby in his or her cot awake, say goodnight, and then quietly leave the room.

✱ **STEP 2** Pour yourself an enormous glass of wine. You're going to need it. Take a big gulp. Baby starts crying. Wait five minutes before going in. Stay for a few minutes to reassure him/her, then say goodnight and leave the room.

✱ **STEP 3** Drink more wine. If baby is still crying after five more minutes, go back in and repeat the process. This time, stand outside the door with your wine and allow yourself to cry. As you cradle your wine, let the tears flow freely.

✱ **STEP 4** Cry hysterically for ten minutes. Pull yourself together and go back in to reassure baby, then come back outside to drink more wine and cry a bit more.

✱ **STEP 5** Repeat the process, but extend the wait between visits by two minutes each time, until either baby or you cry yourselves to sleep.

(BARELY) CONTROLLED CRYING

The Parkinson's Technique

My youngest son, Wilf, went through a phase as a baby of just not sleeping. Ever. He would cry and cry, but would not sleep for more than twenty minutes at a go. I tried everything I could think of: controlled crying, rocking him in his pushchair, driving him around for hours in the car, cuddling him, but nothing seemed to work. I was at my wits' end. Then one day I dropped by with the boys to see my dad and his girlfriend. Wilfie was screaming his head off as usual and I plonked him in my dad's arms, saying, 'Here – take your grandson, please.' Then suddenly, as if by magic, everything went quiet. Wilfie stopped crying and, oh my God, he'd actually broken into a little smile. A moment of glorious, golden silence. You see, my dad suffers from Parkinson's Disease and his relentlessly shaking arms must have calmed Wilf down. He was being shaken vigorously and quickly, his chubby cheeks rippling with the vibration, and he absolutely loved it! He chortled and squealed with delight and then suddenly fell into a deep sleep. Gina Ford – stick that in your pipe and smoke it!

Real Parents' Top Five Ways to Survive Sleep Deprivation

* **Caffeine.**
  In all forms. Coffee, Coca-Cola, chocolate – get as much down your throat as possible. Without it you won't survive. Don't be afraid of dependency – you can learn to love your addiction as it becomes part of you.

* **Bake cakes.**
  It will take your mind off your exhaustion, doesn't require much concentration and will provide the perfect accompaniment to the copious amounts of coffee you will consume. All cakes should be coffee-based: coffee and

walnut cake, chocolate and coffee gateau,
coffee cream cake, triple coffee sponge.

✱ **Write a quirky children's story.**
You are teetering on the edge of insanity and
will be able to create the most surreal, weird
tales, which kids will adore. How do you
think J. K. Rowling managed it?

✱ **Put the kids in the car and drive around until they fall asleep.**
Then pull over somewhere quiet and have a
nap yourself. Be careful not to stop anywhere
too remote and out of the way. A passer-by
may think you've gassed yourself and the kids
and then try to save you. That would be a bit
embarrassing.

✱ **Try to imagine you have just been on a nine-hour flight from Barbados.**
That way you can convince yourself that
your permanent sensation of jetlag is the
consequence of a wonderful holiday and you
won't feel so bad. (OK, this one is lame, I'll admit.
But hey, I'm tired too – what do you expect?

6. MUMMY MADNESS

Mumnesia

As any mother knows, when your baby finally comes out into the big wide world, a little bit of your brain falls out too. Tiny little fragments of sanity are left lying on the grubby hospital floor. The result is that new mothers often misplace things, forget what they are searching for and have total lapses of memory. It's OK, ladies – say it loud and say it proud: 'I've got Mumnesia and I'm completely and utterly mental.'

In the first few months after the birth of both of my boys, I found myself pouring milk into the kettle, putting dirty nappies into the fridge and carefully loading cutlery into the washing machine. All women expect to go a bit la-la after the birth of a baby, but the thing about Mumnesia is that it can last well beyond those first few months. It can last weeks or months or even (yikes!) – dare I say it? – years.

Real Parents' Top Five Examples of Extended Mumnesia

 'One of the best sounds in the world is your own child laughing, and my three-year-old son found it hysterically funny if I put his pants on my head. It was also a great way to get him dressed for nursery, as he would be so distracted that he would forget to kick up a fuss. I'm sure you can guess what happened next. Yes, I forgot to remove the hilarious garment and took my son to nursery with a pair of Sportacus pants on my head. The worst thing is that it wasn't an isolated incident – I have arrived at nursery decked in toddler pants on a number of occasions.'

 'We were running late for a kid's birthday party so I frantically wrote the card, wrapped the present and got my son ready to go out.

Then I had one of those annoying moments when I just couldn't find one of his shoes. I rushed round the house looking everywhere I could think of, including the bin (where it had turned up a few times before). As we were so late, I had to give up the shoe hunt and my son had to wear his wellies to the party. The next day I had a slightly bemused phone call from the mother of the birthday boy, thanking me for the dirty shoe that I had wrapped and given to her son. I seriously worry that my sanity has left me for ever. I need special care or something.'

'I'm a GP, and when my eldest child was about two and a half and my youngest was five months, I think I was at my most emotionally unstable. Which was bad news for my patients, seeing that I was back at work. One Monday, after I'd had a particularly sleepless and stressful weekend of teething and potty training, an elderly patient came in complaining of haemorrhoids. I looked at him sympathetically and said, "Oh pumpkin, let's get you some cream for your sore botty-bum-bum." As soon as the words came out of my mouth I almost wet myself with embarrassment.'

 'One morning, my husband and I were both running very late for work. We were madly trying to get ourselves and our toddler dressed, packing our work bags, tripping over the dog and spilling tea. It was chaos and I really needed to dash if I wanted to get our daughter to nursery in time to catch my train. I kissed my husband goodbye and drove off. When I arrived at the nursery door, I was greeted with a puzzled look by a member of staff. I suddenly became aware that my daughter was nowhere to be seen, but my dog was standing eagerly beside me. I had taken Miffy to nursery. When I got back home, my husband was standing in the driveway holding our daughter. He passed her to me without smiling and just said, "You're a fucking loony." He was right.'

'It was my first day back at work after the birth of my third child and I was thoroughly enjoying myself. So much so, in fact, that I took a moment to close my eyes and listen to the sound of people tapping on their keyboards and mumbling on the phone. Not a single cry from a baby or shout of "Mummy" or sound of a horrible noisy toy. It was bliss. I sat back, soaking up the grown-up office sounds for a good few minutes. I was so lost in the moment that I completely forgot where I was and suddenly shouted, "God, I love it here!" And then I stood up and pushed out the loudest fart I think I have ever done. I don't know what came over me. The office fell silent and everyone turned to stare at me, so I quickly threw myself under my desk to hide. I spent ten minutes under there before I plucked up the courage to get back to my work. Farting in public is totally out of character for me.'

7. POO

Talking Shit

From the moment our new baby pops into the world, we parents are conditioned into obsessing about poo. We wait eagerly for baby's first meconium poo and whoop with delight when it finally emerges. We marvel in wonder as baby's poo gradually changes appearance, from sticky green tar to squishy chicken korma. What a clever baby! It's a joy to behold and nothing short of a miracle! It's pooptastic!!

Of course, non-parents think we are completely mental with our constant talk of turds. And why wouldn't they? Because, let's face it, we *have* gone mental. And this is partly due to the amount of shit we have to deal with on a day-to-day basis. It's never-ending. Nappies for two years, then potty training, then toilet training, then just when you think your days might be shit free, you hear the dreaded cry 'I'VE FINISHED' and realize that you will now be facing a stinky, naked, waving bottom two or three times a day for the foreseeable future. Oh the joy.

But on the plus side, parents consequently learn a new skill. You – yes, *you*, my fellow parent – can now proudly refer to yourself as a Turd Expert. A Professor of Poo. There is no shit that you haven't seen and no plop that can unnerve you. And for that reason, you are best qualified to compile the real parents' poo chart.

Real Parents' Poo Chart

The golden nugget. 'This is a special poo and my own personal favourite. In a nappy it comes out as a soft, golden ball and in the toilet as a soft, golden sausage. Its odour is non-offensive and just one wipe will do the job. It truly is a little treasure.'

The raisin poo. 'This is a revolting poo. It comes from over-feeding your child raisins, which they swallow whole and which then reappear in perfect form. They get everywhere and I hate them.'

The Malteser poo. 'Small, round and solid – one once rolled out of my son's nappy and disappeared under the sofa and I never found it again. I presume the cat ate it.'

The poo explosion. 'An upset-tummy poo of Titanic and windy proportions.'

The 'What the fuck is that?' poo. 'These poos scare me, where an unidentified object appears in the poo. I once found a tiny farmyard pig in my son's nappy. It was a plastic pig, not a real one, by the way.'

The angel poo. 'Every parent's dream poo – a poo so perfect that it doesn't need wiping.'

The squirter. 'Sometimes my newborn son could fire one about three feet, leaving whoever was changing him screaming to the other one, "He's done a squirter, quick, help!" whilst sitting there still holding his legs in the air, covered in yellow poo.'

Moon and stars poo. 'My three-year-old son did a couple of poos in his potty – one was longish and curled slightly and the other was small and ball-like. He shouted out,

"Mum, I have done a moon and star poo," and actually, to be fair, they were shaped like that! So now, if he does two or more poos in one go, they are officially named moon and stars poos!'

 The Johnny Wilkinson. 'My daughter used to do these when she was in nappies. She would stand leaning forward with her hands clasped together and knees slightly bent, then would utter "nggggg" while she tried to push it out. Thankfully she didn't try to score a penalty goal when her turd plopped out.'

 The blue poo. 'I once gave my one-year-old a punnet of blueberries to keep her occupied whilst I was on the phone. She ate the whole lot. When she filled her nappy a few hours later, I was horrified to see that her poo was blue. I've never heard of blue poo before. I think it's quite rare. A bit like blue flowers – they're quite rare too, aren't they?'

Enough of this shit. Let's move on.

8. GENITALS

Bits 'n' Pieces

Question: when is a penis not a penis? Answer: when it's a diddle. You see, somewhere along the way in the great big world of parenting, you have to decide what to call your children's genitals. Now, politically correct, right-on parents will sneer and say, 'What's the problem? The male and female genitalia have their own correct anatomical names, so why not use them?'

Well, with boy's bits there isn't such a huge problem. When Oscar first started to question what he had in his pants, I instinctively called it a penis. I wasn't trying to be politically correct or make a statement – I just didn't think that 'penis' was an offensive word. If I had a penis, I'd call it a penis. Jim, on the other hand, thinks that it's a bit of a harsh word for a three-year-old to use, so he calls it a 'willy'. As a result, Oscar now thinks that he has a penis *and* a willy.

Substitute penis names are fairly standard, with the more prosaic terms having prevailed and stood the test of time. 'Willy', 'winkie', 'dinkie', 'pee-pee' and 'tiddler' are the most popular terms. But some parents are a little more creative:

Real Parents' Top Five Willy-Replacement Names

* **Wiggly Woo.** (*Named after the worm at the bottom of the garden.*)
* **Fireman Sam.** (*I can only presume that this is a reference to a fire hose, rather than suggesting that Fireman Sam looks like a penis.*)
* **Trunk.** (*Does that mean Elmer has two trunks?*)
* **Pinkie Dinky Doo.** (*For those not in the know, Pinkie Dinky Doo is a cartoon girl who appears on CBeebies. Yes, I know, it makes me feel uncomfortable too.*)
* **Magic wand.** (*Will make you read Harry*

Potter in a totally different light! 'Stand up and take out your wand, Potter,' said Professor Snape.)

With girls' bits, it becomes a little more complex and it's much easier to hide behind a euphemism. Not necessarily because we are uncomfortable with female sexual anatomy or want to belittle feminism. No, it's because women's rude bits are so very complicated – an assemblage of muddled, interconnected body parts that requires a cohesive, colloquial name.

Responsible, grown-up parents might well refer to their daughter's downstairs region as her vagina. But they are anatomically wrong. The vagina is the internal tract only; the outside parts of the female reproductive organs include the vulva, labia and clitoris. I have a friend whose four-year-old daughter proudly and accurately refers to her specific lady parts, which is very clever, I'm sure. But I found myself wincing with discomfort when we were all quietly reading books at the local library and she shouted at the top of her voice, 'Mummy, my labia is sore.' Those aren't the kind of words you want to hear coming from the mouth of an innocent cherub. But neither are the euphemisms commonly used for an adult's genitalia. It's hardly appropriate for a little girl to be referring to her fanny, muff, punani or pussy, is it? So a generic, non-offensive word is a necessity. I asked a random selection of parents from nurseries and playgroups to share their child-friendly vagina euphemisms. Some of their answers were very . . . er . . . 'creative'!

Real Parents' Top Ten Fanny-Replacement Names

* **Mary.** (*This is the most popular replacement name. Is it a religious reference? Not very respectful, is it?*)
* **Wendy.** (*What's the deal with using girls' names? And why Wendy? Why not Elizabeth or Rachel or Maud?*)
* **Minny.** (*One little girl innocently said to her mother, 'Mummy, do eggs come from an Easter bunny's minny?' Her mum replied, 'Yes, they do.' The little girl paused for a moment and then said, 'Is that why they're called Mini Eggs?'*)
* **Fluffy.** (*Why you would choose to use the name of a pet guinea pig, I do not know.*)

* **Worzel.** (*As in the TV scarecrow Worzel Gummidge. That's a bit disturbing, isn't it?*)
* **Nonny.** (*'With a hey, and a ho, and a hey nonino' Shakespeare loved his nonnies.*)
* **Perkin.** (*Paying homage to seventies kids' TV show* The Flumps? *Actually, Flump is a fantastic fanny-replacement name. And so, for that matter, are Posey and Pootle. And Flumpet is a great willy-replacement name.*)
* **Tuppence.** (*Is that really all it's worth?*)
* **Luv.** (*Had top-ten hit with 'Shout' and can do a great cover of Bowie's 'Man Who Sold The World'.*)
* **Poochie.** (*Eighties toy poodle with curly hair and pink ears that could do extraordinary things. Sounds about right.*)

Hey Fiddle Fiddle!

Once kids have discovered that there is something hidden under their pants that they were previously unaware of, they become obsessed with it. Young girls habitually rummage around at any opportunity, usually at an embarrassingly inappropriate moment. During the wonderful pre-school years, children are so unaffected and innocent that the most unintentionally awkward scenarios can occur. One mummy recalls the time she took her kids to McDonald's and had to make a hasty exit after her four-year-old daughter pulled down her knickers, held up her summer dress and attempted to feed her cheeseburger to her 'minny' because it was apparently 'very hungry'.

N.B. Always make a note of these moments as they can be used as ammunition to embarrass your teenage kids in the future.

Boys tend to discover their penis within the first year of life and take great delight in playing with it whenever they get the opportunity. They bend and contort it in ways you wouldn't know were possible. I've seen Oscar stretch his penis like a piece of elastic to such a length that I worried he might damage the ligament (does a penis have ligaments? I don't know – I'm not a penis expert) so it wouldn't return to its normal size. I had visions of Oscar as a twenty-five-year-old man having to explain to his partner that the reason his penis dragged on the floor was because of vigorous childhood tugging.

Shortly after boys realize they have something between their legs, they appear to develop an overwhelming desire to put it in things. Usually dangerous things.

Top Five Places Little Boys Have Put Their Willies

- Through the cat flap.
- Down the plug hole.
- In the cat's ear.
- In a toy teapot spout (where it got stuck and had to be removed at A&E).
- In a plug socket.

Warning: Winkies Can Tip You Over the Edge

Jim and I once took the boys on a particularly stressful family holiday to Centre Parcs. Wilfie was about seven months old and Oscar was coming up to three, and I was exhausted, tense and longing for some time alone. We were all squeezed into a family changing room at the swimming pool – Oscar was playing up, Wilfie was screaming his head off and Jim was getting annoyed. They were all naked, whilst I was still fully dressed. And it was at this moment that I had a meltdown. The shouting and screaming got louder and louder, there were naked male bodies all around me and I began to feel really claustrophobic. The walls began to close in on me. Too many penises in one little space. I was outnumbered by willies and couldn't cope. A waggle of winkies (for that is the collective noun) had triggered a panic attack.

9. BABY TALK

The Language of the Playgroup

One thing many of us fear about becoming a parent is attending playgroups. We imagine a room full of snot-encrusted kids, screaming and throwing battered old toys at one another whilst their mums (and a scattering of dads) chat about poo with smelly coffee breath and spit biscuit crumbs all over each other. But however awful the prospect of playgroup is, it's still a much better option than the alternative: to stay at home. When you spend the day at home alone with children, the minutes drag and the hours can last for ever. The kids get bored and ratty, you start to lose the will to live and everyone ends up screaming and/or crying.

Playgroup, then, is definitely the lesser of the two evils. But before you enter the battleground you must learn the language of the playgroup. It's kind of like a code and is undoubtedly tough to crack, but once you've mastered it, you'll find the whole playgroup scene much easier to handle. So here are a few handy hints from real mummies to help you:

Language of the Playgroup	Translation
'Gosh, he's a big boy.'	*'What a fat porker.'*
'He's very lively, isn't he?'	*'Your son is a little shit.'*
'She doesn't look anything like her big brother.'	*'She's much uglier than her big brother.'*
'I'm really tired.'	*'Please don't talk to me.'*
'Well, they all develop at different rates.'	*'Your child is backward.'*
'Wow, you're *still* breastfeeding?'	*'You repulse me.'*
'Oh, are you the nanny?'	*'You'll never understand what I'm going through. Now please fuck off.'*
'Are you tired?'	*'You look like shit.'*
'So are you good friends with Kathy?'	*'I'm about to slag off Kathy.'*

'She's got a good pair of lungs on her.'	*'Shut your child up, for God's sake.'*
'Do you use the naughty step?'	*'Your child is completely out of control.'*
'What does your husband do?'	*'Are you rich?'*
'Is that Alfie's muslin?'	*'Your thieving brat has just nicked my child's favourite blankie.'*
'She looks like a little pixie.'	*'She has massive ears.'*
'Well, it definitely isn't my son.'	*'Your child has done a big, stinky poo.'*

10. MUSIC

Kid Rock

No one tells you what a significant role music will play in the first few years of your child's life. It's a fundamental communication tool. From lullabies to nursery rhymes, from television programmes to toys, music is an integral part of a child's early years. So let's take a look at the key musical stages for young children.

Lullabies

Be honest. How many traditional lullabies do you know? Off the top of my head, I can name one – 'Rock-a-bye Baby'. But does my lack of lullaby knowledge officially make me a failure as a parent? I do sing to my boys at bedtime, but not lullabies as such. Instead, I warble my way through a selection of rock and pop ballads, from Led Zeppelin's 'Stairway To Heaven' to Chris Isaak's 'Wicked Game' (which is very tricky to sing – try it and see). It rarely sends them off to sleep. In fact, it has become more of a game, with Oscar regarding me as a kind of night-time juke-box providing instant requests. 'Do Meatloaf, Mummy. It's funny!' OK, so 'I Would Do Anything For Love (But I Won't Do That)' is hardly comparable to 'Hush Little Baby' (had to Google that one), but at least I give it a shot! A recent survey found that 89 per cent of parents would rather play music on the radio or a CD to their children at bedtime than sing to them. What a cop out!

Nursery Rhymes

Music groups are a favourite weekly activity for many toddlers and parents. Everyone starts off sitting in a circle whilst the group leader enthusiastically steers the parents and children through a series of nursery rhymes. I remember taking Oscar to a group once, when he was about eight months old and fast asleep. Try as I might, I could not wake him up, so I ended up awkwardly singing 'Incy Wincy Spider' (with actions) to a zonked-out baby lying limply on the floor in front of me. To make matters worse, one of the other mummies took pity on me and since her toddler was more interested in twisting himself up in the church-hall curtains, she decided to use me as her 'Row, Row, Row the Boat' partner. It was one of the most horrible experiences of my life.

Toys

All parents hate toys that take batteries, because a) the batteries will at some point run out, which will cause your child to whinge or throw a temper tantrum, and b) toys with batteries are noisy.

To begin with, I had an agreement with

all my mummy friends that we wouldn't give 'noisy toys' as gifts. Then gradually, as mummy madness crept in, it became sadistically amusing to try and outdo each other with louder and louder presents. Our house transmits a constant audio medley of singing books, talking teddies, beeping lorries, emergency sirens and noisy space-rocket launch pads. I remember being woken suddenly at three a.m. one night by a sleepy voice from the end of our bed purring, 'Oooh, it's rather nice to have a cuddle.' It scared the hell out of Jim, who screamed like a girl and adopted a defensive karate stance on the bed (which is a strange instinctive thing to do, seeing as he knows nothing about martial arts). Who left bloody Bagpuss under the duvet?

Noisy toys are horrible. In a recent survey, Deafness Research UK tested a range of toys and found that fourteen out of fifteen produced noise levels above the recommended safety limit when held close to the ear. Sod the kids – these toys should come with a set of ear plugs for the poor parents.

TV Songs

Songs on children's TV have always been able to worm their way into your brain, where they play on a continual loop, getting faster and faster, until you fear your head may explode. But music on television for pre-school kids has come a long way since we were subjected to the likes of *Playaway* and Rod, Jane and Freddy. The songs that feature on CBeebies and Milkshake are not only incredibly catchy, but, dare I say it, actually quite brilliant.

Nowhere in the vast array of parenting handbooks available in all good bookshops is there any kind of warning that parents of pre-schoolers will actively start enjoying kids' TV theme tunes on the basis of their own musical merits. I'll be honest with you – I have downloaded CBeebies songs to my Ipod. If I press Shuffle, it's quite likely that the theme tune to *Space Pirates* will crop up in between The Kings of Leon and Prince. And it doesn't sound out of place. So next time you are absent-mindedly singing, 'Yes, my name is Iggle

Piggle' whilst squeezing melons in Sainsbury's, remember that you're probably not the only one.

How to Influence Your Child's Musical Taste

Music does weird things to people. Even the most liberal-minded parents, who would never dream of forcing religious views or political opinions on their children, will forcefully attempt to impose their own musical tastes on them. Ask yourself this: are you a parental music fascist? I know I am.

It's a fact – most kids' songs (with the exception of a few fantastic TV theme tunes) really get on your nerves. I mean, let's face it, does any parent really get any pleasure from singing all seventy-four verses of 'The Wheels On The Bus'? No, because it's a truly terrible song. Of course, kids love repetition and rhyme, but if you sprinkle on a few other magical musical ingredients you'll find that they will warm to a whole range of musical genres.

Key Ingredients for the Perfect Child-Friendly Song

* **Animals.** Any pop song that mentions an animal will automatically be a favourite, e.g. Tom Jones, 'What's New Pussy Cat?'
* **Sweetness.** With music, as with food, children are sugar fiends. They love simple melodies, chirpy voices and catchy choruses, e.g. S Club 7, 'Reach For The Stars'.
* **Shouting.** Children are constantly looking for any excuse to be noisy, so any song with shouting is always going to go down well, e.g. Billy Idol, 'Mony Mony'.

Long car journeys can be dreadful when you just want to listen to your new Coldplay album but fear risking a full-on five-star temper tantrum if you don't play *The Greatest Nursery Rhymes Ever* on a continual loop. I mean, it's not entirely unreasonable to want to drive off a cliff after hearing 'Wind The Fucking Bobbin Up' on the car CD player for the hundreth time, is it? But fear not, I've come up with a way to satisfy both your child's and your own groovy musical tastes: create a playlist that features bands and artists you love (or at least tolerate), playing songs the kids love too. That way, you can try to subliminally influence your child's taste in music. It's a cunning plan and everyone's a winner.

Real Parents' Top Ten Tried and Tested Cool Songs That Kids Love

* **The Wonder Stuff, 'The Size Of A Cow'.** Just the mention of a cow is enough to make children love this song.

* **David Bowie, 'The Laughing Gnome'.** Either a work of genius or total rubbish – it's a fine line.

* **Sultans of Ping FC, 'Where's Me Jumper?'** A really great, perennial student-night, shouty, sing-a-long song.

* **Toy Dolls, 'Nellie The Elephant'.** A very cool punk reworking of the old classic, loved by both kids and parents.

* **Madonna, 'Holiday'.** Madonna may now be a wrinkly old dear in a leotard, with a camel's toe, but you can't go wrong with her early stuff.

* **Toni Basil, 'Mickey'.** Surely one of the best and most catchy pop songs of the eighties.

* **The Cure, 'Love Cats'.** Ah! Pussy cats. Meow!

* **Beatles, 'Yellow Submarine'.** The most rubbish Beatles song ever. But it's still the Beatles, I guess.

* **Fuzzbox, 'Pink Sunshine'.** Cor blimey! A blast from the past. Four bonkers girls with dodgy hair, who had a top-twenty hit with this catchy, punky pop track.

* **All Seeing Eye, 'Walk Like A Panther'.** Super-slinky, super-cool Tony Christie, singing about panthers, eagles, salmons and lions. Much better than 'The Animals Went In Two By Two'.

Music –
Parental Advisory Warning

There will be a few occasions when your kids will be so preoccupied with toys that they will allow you to listen to the radio or play a CD of your choice. (Lucky you!) And it is at these precise moments that you will forget that children are like sponges – soaking up everything that is going on in the background, including the music they hear.

It's not as if you'll deliberately put N.W.A.'s 'Fuck Tha Police' or The Prodigy's 'Smack My Bitch Up' on the stereo, but sometimes you will unintentionally expose your child to music that is totally inappropriate. And you can guarantee that these are the songs that will stick in their innocent little minds. These songs are subtle but dangerous. Tracks that appear on your favourite album, or pop songs that get played on the radio – have you ever stopped and really listened to their lyrical content to ascertain their suitability? No? Then you are a very naughty parent indeed.

11. TELEVISION

TV or Not TV?

Everyone knows that the most evil thing a parent can do is to allow their kids to watch television. Hardly a week goes by without some report reminding us of the debilitating effects of sticking the kids in front of the box. Too much television will lead to attention-deficit disorder, eye problems, obesity, premature puberty, ultimately unsociable behaviour, blah, blah, blah. So in years to come, when your four-eyed, fat, hairy, hyperactive, socially retarded teenager violently attacks an innocent stranger with a move they learnt from Boogie Pete, you'll only have yourself to blame.

But we all know that six to seven p.m. is the witching hour. The children are tired, ratty and don't know what to do with themselves. So they throw themselves around, stick things in plug sockets, scream, cry, put pencils up the cat's bum and try to shut each other's fingers in the door. The only way to calm things down is to put on CBeebies to zone them out. And it works. So you see, children's TV is a vital tool for parents.

But I urge you to think carefully before you too chill out on the sofa in front of children's TV. It can be very dangerous. With the repetitive music and hypnotic, psychedelic colours swirling about on the screen, it's easy to forget that you are tired, emotional and mentally weak. You might think you're innocently watching Lazy Town, but as your feeble mind begins to wander, suddenly you're having erotic visions of Sportacus doing one-armed press-ups on your sitting-room rug, wearing nowt but his goggles and moustache. And that is WRONG!

Pretty female children's presenters have been the source of dads' pervy fantasies for decades. But there was no one except for John Craven, Geoffrey from *Rainbow* and Terry Nutkins for our mums to drool over when we were kids. (Yuck!)

Want some SPORTS CANDY?

Fast-forward twenty years and suddenly there's something for everyone. And it turns out that mummy eye-candy is different from normal eye-candy. Mummies are mental. They're not looking for tall, dark and handsome, because they realize that's not realistic. No gorgeous hunk of a man will look twice at a knackered, neurotic, saggy and mentally unstable mother. So what mummies want to see is a cheeky glint of an eye, a knowing smile, a little bit of naughty humour. And that's it. Bingo. A nation of leering mummy perverts are glued to the box.

Real Mummies' Top Ten CBeebies Sex Fantasies

* **Chris Corcoran,** presenter of *Doodle Doo*. 'He looks mega strict and I find that a real turn-on. I'd like him to bang me with those furry-creature glove puppets on his hands.'
* **Big Cook Little Cook.** 'Together, at the same time, with Little Cook the same tiny size as he is on TV, so he can crawl into the important places.'
* **Boogie Pete** from *Boogie Beebies*. 'Naked and back-flipping off my kitchen units whilst I watch and eat chocolate mousse.'

* **Mr Tumble**. 'I'd like to see him orgasm in sign language.'
* **Captain DJ** from *Space Pirates*. 'I think he's far more sexy than Johnny Depp in *Pirates of the Caribbean*. I've fantasized about him rubbing his moustache all over my body.'
* **Sarah Jane Honeywell** from *Tikkabilla*. 'I'd like to see her with a strap-on. She looks like she wants it.'
* **The Wiggles**. 'In a four–one gang bang. But Murray the red one looks a bit creepy, so I wouldn't want his spindly hands on my tits.'
* **Sid**, the CBeebies presenter. 'I think about him dancing naked on a white fur rug in a ski chalet singing the CBeebies winter song.'
* **Archie** from *Balamory*. 'He looks like he has a massive cock under that kilt. I can tell by the size of his hands.'
* **Roma** from *The Hoobs*. 'I know she's a puppet, but I also think she might be a lesbian and I find that quite alluring. Do you know if she is a lesbian? No? Can you find out?'

Real Daddies' Top Ten CBeebies Sex Fantasies

* *Sarah Jane Honeywell* in *Higgledy House*. 'She is so sexy. And she seems really mischievous, like she'd be really naughty. She also looks a bit like a little goblin – you know, a really hot, sexy little goblin. No, I'm not saying that she actually resembles a green goblin, I'm just saying that she's really sexy in a goblin-like way. Not that I want to shag a goblin, but do you know what I mean?' (*Congratulations and ten sexy CBeebies bonus points awarded to Sarah Jane for appearing in both Mummies' and Daddies' lists. A great achievement!*)

* *Nina* from *Nina and the Neurons*. 'Oh, Nina's great, isn't she? She's like a young Claire Grogan. Sexy smile, sexy voice and those kinky 'fuck me' boots. She's my guilty wank.'

* *Aunty Mabel* from *Come Outside*. 'I love a bossy woman. I can imagine her in a PVC catsuit and it makes me feel all funny.'

* **Miss Hoolie** from *Balamory*. 'She's just so very sexy. I love her flicked-out hair and her long sexy eyelashes. It's very obvious to me that she and PC Plum have a passionate desire for one another. I like to imagine that when no one is looking they bang each other senseless in the nursery cupboard.'

* **Cerrie Burnell**, CBeebies presenter. 'It's not the fact that she's got one arm, it's just that she's totally gorgeous and talented. She's wasted on kids' TV. She should be somewhere where all men can admire her beauty. Like BBC 1 or page 3 of the *Sun*.'

* **Carrie Grant** from *Carrie and David's Popshop*. 'She's a fox. Those stiletto heels and skin-tight jeans she wears on every show are purely for the benefit of us sex-deprived dads. No wonder David Grant looks so smug when he's married to such a minx. Lucky bastard.'

* **Granny Murray** from *Me Too!* 'She's got a look about her that says, "I'll take no shit from you, sonny Jim," and she's got an amazing rack that I just want to bury my head in.'

* *Pui Fan Lee* from *Show Me Show Me*. 'She's so beautiful and lovely. I adore her and so does my two-year-old son. He's got great taste in women, just like me. Pui is so kind and sweet, I bet even her snot tastes of sugar. I'd happily eat it.'

* *Suzie Sweet* from *Balamory*. 'I know she's an older woman with helmet hair but I find her extremely attractive. If you imagine Suzie Sweet dressed in a little boy's school uniform she'd look a bit like Jimmy Krankie. Don't you think? Does that make me sound weird?'

* *Upsy Daisy* from *In the Night Garden*. 'I don't fancy her or anything weird, I just think she looks really snugly and cuddly so I'd love to hug her tight. Don't worry, it's nothing sexual, although I suppose if the cuddle were to lead to other things then I'd probably go along with it. So yes, OK, I'd shag Upsy Daisy. But can I just stress that I really don't fancy her?'

12. CHRISTMAS

Ho Ho Ho

Nothing puts the magic back into Christmas quite like your own children. Even the grumpiest, most Scrooge-like parent can't help but get swept along by the enchanted wave of excitement that kids ride throughout December, and there is absolutely no denying that seeing Christmas through the eyes of a pre-schooler is one of the most joyful experiences ever. Everything that you have always hated and couldn't understand about Christmas suddenly makes sense. In the past I have watched in amazement as two grown women furiously wrestled over a Buzz Lightyear action figure in the Disney Store. I just didn't get it. What on earth were they doing? *Now* I understand – I too would violently rugby-tackle any like-minded parent in Mothercare who was just about to grab the last all-singing, all-dancing Iggle Piggle on the shelf.

But all this excitement comes at a cost. A week or so before Christmas, most kids are verging on overload. The prospect of chocolate, presents and Father Christmas arriving on his sleigh is enough to send any child into a total frenzy. The anticipation is a pretty tough challenge for them. And of course, as a good, caring, sensible parent, you would never exploit your child's innocent excitement, would you? You wouldn't do that. To foresee a whole month of potential good behaviour and then carefully plan a system of Dickensian threats and bribes to make sure you got it – well, that would just be cruel. Wait! What's that in your Christmas stocking? A lump of coal? Someone's been naughty . . .

Real Parents' Top Five Father Christmas Threats

 'For the entire December run-up to Christmas, I tell my children that Father Christmas is watching their every move. He has CCTV set up in every room of the house and won't tolerate any bad behaviour. Naughtiness equals no presents. Father Christmas is Big Brother. My kids are scared stiff of him. December in my house usually passes by with perfectly behaved kids. Mission accomplished.' (*N.B. Evil parent will pay for this when poor children become stroppy teenagers. Revenge will be sweet.*)

♀ 'My daughters believe that Father Christmas has a special radar that picks up the vibrations that are made when they pick their bogies and eat them. I know it has totally freaked them out as they now only eat their bogies underneath their duvets at night where they believe that the radar can't reach them.' (*Bogey prohibition will only lead to it being pushed underground.*)

♂ 'Last year, when I was at my wits' end on Christmas Eve, I said something bad. I told my little boy that every time he did something naughty, one of Father Christmas's tiny elves would die.' (*A serial killer at just four years old? Imagine growing up with that on your conscience.*)

♀ 'My three-year-old daughter somehow got it into her head that if Father Christmas found out you had been naughty, he'd send Rudolf down the chimney and into your bedroom to do a big poo on your head. I never told her that this wasn't true, so on Christmas Eve she fell asleep in her bed with a toy teapot on her head to protect her.' (*And they say that anticipation is the best part of Christmas!*)

 'When I was a little girl, I used to tell my younger brother that if he didn't go to sleep on Christmas Eve, Father Christmas would come into his room, chop off his willy and put it in his stocking instead of his presents. As a result my brother was petrified of Father Christmas. You will be happy to know that I haven't used the same threat on my two little boys. Yet!' (*Arrrrrrgh!*)

The Cattle Are Blowing the Baby Away

Surely the sweetest Christmas carol to be sung by children is 'Away In A Manger'. I was delighted when Oscar broke into a spontaneous rendition in the back of our car as we were on our way home from nursery. My little boy, all excited about Christmas, singing joyfully with his sweet and angelic voice:

> 'Away in a manger,
> No crib for a bed,
> The little whore Jesus
> Lay down his sweet head.'

No! That's not right! When I mentioned this awkward moment to my mum, she told me that when I was at pre-school I came home enthusing about a new song I'd learned called 'The Cheetah Song'. She had no idea what I was on about until I started singing 'Away In A Manger', and 'the little Lord Jesus' became 'the little Lor Cheetah'. Ah, of course.

Real Children's Top Five 'Little Lord Jesus' Misheard Lyrics

* The little Lord Cheesy.
* The little Lord Jizz-whiz.
* The little low genie.
* The little Malteser.
* The little Sore Penis.

Festive Fun

Christmas is a time for family. A time for creating those precious, snapshot moments that can be stored happily in your memory for the rest of your life. A time when you and your child can revel in creativity and culture, and immerse yourselves in the wonders of nature. Or some such bollocks.

Real Parents' Top Ten Things You Are Supposed to Enjoy Doing with Your Children at Christmas but Don't

 Christmas-card making. 'Glitter. It drives me nuts. I can't tell you how much I hate making glittery Christmas cards with my daughter. She, of course, loves it and I let her go crazy with the glue and glitter whenever she wants, but I would honestly rather staple my face to a piece of paper and pretend to be Santa Claus than use the glitter. No matter how careful you are with the stuff it still manages to get everywhere: all over the floor, on the furniture, in your hair, on your face, on the frigging cats and pretty much everyfuckingwhere.'

Visiting Father Christmas. 'To ask a small child to go up to a strange old man and sit on his lap is not something we would even consider at any other time of the year. While my daughter is getting bounced up and down on Santa's knee in the department-store grotto, all I can think is "Get your filthy hands off my child, you nonce."'

Going to the church Nativity. 'I love going to church at Christmas, but although I feel guilty saying it, I hate taking my kids. They totally ruin it for everyone. They are noisy, they don't pay attention and my eldest always breaks wind during the quiet bits.'

Ice skating. 'Why would I want to spend half an hour in the freezing cold, endlessly picking my child up from a slippery floor until her bottom gets so wet and numb that she starts crying and doesn't stop for the next two hours? In what way is that fun?'

 Opening Advent calendars. 'When I was a child I used to love opening my Advent-calendar door and was genuinely satisfied when a Nativity scene or a Christmas tree was revealed. These days you can only seem to buy calendars with chocolate behind each door, so I have to watch my son greedily tear open the door and shovel the chocolate into his massive gob as fast as he can. I get no pleasure from watching my child behave like a fat hog at Christmas.'

 Decorating the tree. 'Before I had children, my Christmas tree was so tasteful and elegant. I was always so proud of it. Now it always looks shit. My son insists that we smother it in revolting tinsel, and of course we have to hang up the bits of tat he has made at nursery. Now I am ashamed when my childless friends come round. Children really mess up my Christmas.'

Making the nursery Christmas-play costume. 'I genuinely thought it would be fun to make my daughter's sheep costume by hand. I'm not too nifty with a needle and thread but I thought I'd give it a go. At the performance, I was so embarrassed when I realized that all the other kids were wearing fantastic costumes bought from shops, and my poor little girl came out on to the stage dressed in a white sheet covered with cotton-wool balls. It was so awful, it looked as if she'd actually made it herself. But at least I tried.'

 Winter walks. 'Nobody warned me that kids just can't handle the cold. No matter how many layers you put on them, no matter how much they run around, they still can't keep warm. You could put their hands in electrically warmed boxing gloves and they would still complain that their fingers hurt. My brisk winter walks in the countryside have been ruined by my children. I am raising a couple of wimps.'

Playing in the snow. 'So it's a beautiful morning with thick crisp virgin snow covering the garden. My four-year-old is so excited she can barely contain herself. I wrap her up cosily in her hat, scarf, gloves, wellies and padded all-in-one, super-warm, zip-up snowsuit, and let her outside to play. Within five minutes she needs a wee, and no matter how quickly I try to unzip the snowsuit, I'm just not fast enough. She wets herself. Every single time.'

 Watching The Snowman. 'On Christmas Eve I snuggled up on the sofa with my three-year-old son to watch *The Snowman* – a magical, Christmassy, fantasy animation. He watched in awe, laughing and dancing and becoming completely engrossed. But the ending almost destroyed him. He's not ready to handle death. What on earth was Raymond Briggs thinking when he decided to kill the Snowman? That film should come with a warning. How am I supposed to explain a dead snowman to a three-year-old?'

13. POST-BABY BODIES

Mother Figure

There's no getting away from it – a woman's body is never the same after childbirth. My boobs went right up to a G cup during my second pregnancy. They were MASSIVE and really quite fabulous. But after I stopped breastfeeding they gradually withered away and now I fear that if I were to have any more children they may just shrivel right up and drop off.

I found my first grey hair when I was inspecting the bags under my eyes in the lift in Mothercare. All the sleepless nights have aged me. I have stretch marks. My C-section scar has left a slight bulge that bothers me. Yes, my body is buggered! But I'm rather proud of my defects. I consider them to be battle scars. I earned that grey hair and I worked bloody hard to get norks as saggy as these.

Real Mummies' Post-Baby Battle Scars

★ 'I have an apron of flesh overhanging a stitched-up Wendy, thanks to my ten-pound baby. I also have saggy tits with stretch marks; what used to be funbags are now saddlebags.' (*Cries at reflection.*)

★ 'Before having my son I was once told I had "champion thrupnies". which I was quite pleased about. They were big, round and pointing in the right direction. But not any more: they're more like a fat cow's udders and I need a hammock to hold the buggers up. And don't even get me started about my fanny. I think it has actually perished due to lack of use.'

★ 'My stomach looks like a road atlas of Great Britain. One particular stretch mark runs a route just like the A303 and if you follow it far enough you'll get to my "Minge of

Stonehenge". Once upon a time it was a ceremonial centre of fertility and celebration. Now it is untouched by man and cordoned off as an ancient historical site.'

✱ 'I swear to God that I have grown jowls since the birth of my second child. It's almost as though my cheeks had some kind of sympathetic reaction to my boobs, which have sagged beyond imagination. I think I'm starting to look like Geoffrey Palmer.'

✱ 'No matter how often I do my pelvic-floor exercises, I still have a slack old bucket fanny.'

✱ 'I grew a moustache when I was pregnant. That pissed me off. And it hasn't gone away. The NHS should pay for the amount of Jolene bleach I've had to buy.'

✱ 'My tummy went straight back to normal after each of my three pregnancies, but my bottom has sagged almost down to the backs of my knees. How does that work? I don't recall carrying babies in my buttocks.'

✱ 'I'm really quite pissed off with whoever had the job of stitching me back up after

> my C-section. The scar is wonky and now it looks as though my pubic hair is a toupee. I feel like a right merkin minny.'

★ 'I've got a rather magnificent muffin top. I'm not ashamed of it, though. In fact I celebrate it. On special occasions I'll wear an outfit that shows off my muffin top, bingo wings, whale tail and camel toe all at once. I'm like an edible beast!'

★ 'My body is F.U.C.K.E.D. Let's run through the check list: Tits? Fucked. Tummy? Fucked. Varicose veins? Fucked. Fanny? Fucked . . . Well, not literally. It's too fucked for fucking.'

Father Figure

After one particularly demanding day when the kids had driven me absolutely bonkers, I put them to bed, got undressed and stood naked in front of the mirror. And I didn't like the reflection I saw staring back at me. It wasn't the old me. There were lumps and lines that weren't there before, and bumps and curves that were missing. I was all wrong. So I turned round to face Jim, who was lying on the bed happily reading his book, and furiously shouted, 'Look what you've done to me! I'm decrepit and wobbly and my boobs are nothing more than a couple of dangling chesticles. And it's all your fault!'

I must have looked completely demented, leaping around before him in the knackerdy doo, but Jim just calmly said, 'Stop being silly. You look gorgeous.'

'Well, you would say that, wouldn't you? You're hardly going to tell me that I'm past my sell-by date, are you?'

'I think you look great. You gave birth to our two gorgeous boys. Your body is amazing.'

'Oh sod off.'

He wasn't going to win. It was my body and it was going to take time for me to come to terms with my new shape. But is Jim alone in his genuine admiration for a post-baby body? What about other dads? What do they think? Well, I asked a selection of real daddies that very question and the general feeling seemed to be that tits are tits and a fanny is a fanny, no matter how saggy or slack they are.

To be honest, I'm not sure whether to take that as a compliment or an insult. Answers on a postcard, please.

14. KIDS' FASHION

Extreme Fashion

The other morning, Oscar got himself dressed (very clever). But whenever he has done this in the past, he has usually forgotten to put on one vital item of clothing, so as a precaution I asked him if he was wearing any pants. He replied, 'No, Mummy, I'm just wearing my penis – are you wearing yours today?' Fair to say, I wasn't expecting that particular response so I said, 'No. My clip-on willy

is in the wash at the moment.' He seemed quite satisfied with my answer and went off to watch CBeebies.

But although the sentiment was entirely innocent, I wouldn't be at all surprised to see children's clip-on willies on sale in the near future. Children's fashion has become a fast-growing phenomenon, and it seems that nothing is out of bounds. You can buy see-through thong panties for girls of four and high-heeled shoes for two-year-olds, and the current trend for 'humorous' kids' T-shirts is really close to the knuckle. So close, in fact, that many parents are asking if they have crossed the boundaries of taste. Thus my question to you is this: are these children's T-shirt slogans an aggressive but intelligent comment on today's social attitudes, or are they just downright offensive? You decide.

Inappropriate T-Shirt Slogans Seen on Real Children's T-Shirts

* All Daddy Wanted Was a Blowjob.
* Daddy's Little Squirt.
* Pardon My Nipple Breath.
* Are You My Daddy?
* Fuck the Milk, Where's the Whisky Tit?
* I Love a Good Spanking.

✱ Mummy Drinks Because I Cry.
✱ I'm Hung Just Like My Dad.
✱ Grandma Smells of Piss.
✱ I'm More of a Boob Man.

Designer Babies

In the last few years, some parents have embraced the increasing popularity of designer-label children's wear. Yes, the super-trendy pre-schooler can be kitted out from head to foot in labels such as Ralph Lauren or Little Marc by Marc Jacobs. Perhaps you might like to fork out £60 for a Baby Dior babygro covered in the Dior logo. Or maybe you'd happily spend £102 on a pair of Versace Young trousers for your eighteen-month-old son. Call me a skinflint if you like, but I simply can't justify spending that amount of money on kids' clothes. I mean, has the world gone mad or am I missing something?

Every parent (and I include myself) faces the strong temptation to use their child as a living Barbie/Ken doll. But baby haute couture is taking the piss. A-list celebrities are dressing their little darlings in ludicrously expensive, baby-size Gucci, Prada and Armani gear. They wouldn't think twice about spending £100 on a Versace baby T-shirt, even though within ten minutes it will be covered in dribble/sick/poo/snot/lunch/milk – and probably all six by the end of the day.

Of course, it's completely understandable that parents want the best for their children, but I almost choked when I discovered that you can buy a white cotton Gucci bib for £60. Why would you do that? *Why?*

Real Parents' Most Expensive Items of Clothing Bought for Their Children (and How They Justify Them)

 'One Sunday, we were going to the children's farm and my four-year-old son James refused to leave the house in anything other than his Christian Dior knitted jumper, which cost me £115 and was intended for special occasions only. To spare us a five-star temper tantrum, I let him wear it. Why he chose that particular day to roll around in a sodding cowpat, I do not know. He's never done it before and never done it since, but the day he wore Dior was the day the jumper died. It actually makes me tearful when I think about it.'

'I bought a beautiful Roberto Cavalli christening gown for £150. I cannot tell you how upset I was when my five-month-old son had an enormous poo explosion in church. Honestly, his whole dress was covered, as were I, my husband and the poor vicar. It was as though my son had saved up his entire life's worth of poo and shat it out on his special day. It was vile. I'm sure even God was retching.'

 'I spent £60 on a Burberry cashmere scarf for my three-year-old daughter. I thought it would last her for years and would keep her warm. You can imagine my horror when I found her one afternoon quietly dunking her scarf into the toilet. When I asked her what she was doing she replied, "I'm catching my poo, Mummy." Unfortunately she has a pretty good aim and her beautiful scarf was indeed cradling her little poo.'

Children's Fashion Faux Pas

These days, of course, there are countless online shops selling trendy children's wear, but in the olden days parents could splash their cash on groovy kiddie clothes from mail-order catalogues. I have a rather unpleasant memory of me, Mum, Dad and my little brother Alex all walking along a windy beach in the pissing rain wearing identical canary-yellow sailing macs that made us look like greased-up bananas. You see, in the early eighties my mum was a loyal customer of the Clothkits catalogue, which specialized in free-spirit, casual clothes that encouraged individuality. But far from allowing us to express our unique taste, she used to buy in bulk and my entire family would often spend a day out together all dressed in matching stripy long-sleeved T-shirts and brightly coloured jogging bottoms. Even after all this time, I still find it difficult to talk about. It scarred me deeply.

You only have to look back in your old family photo albums to see the hideous mistakes your parents made when they dressed you as a child. I cringe with shame when I think that I used to leave the house wearing a velour, turquoise, zip-up jumpsuit. It might well have been practical and easy to wash, but it made me look like a right numpty. My mum had great fashion sense, so assuming she didn't dress me in the dark, I can't help but wonder what on earth she was thinking. And if she could do it to me, could I do it to my kids? So before you point the finger at other parents' bad fashion judgement, ask yourself this: are you inflicting the same pain and embarrassment on your own children?

Real Parents' Kiddie Fashion Gripes

 'I can't stand it when toddlers have their ears pierced. It's so common. And what kind of example does it set? I mean, ears pierced at eighteen months, nose pierced at four years old, belly button pierced at six, bollocks pierced at eight? Where does it all end? Then it'll be tattoos all over their bodies and one of those CD plates in their mouth like Sting's friend who lived in the rainforest.' (*Just imagine that. Press little Josh's nose and Sting's* Ten Summoner's Tales *album will eject from his mouth.*)

 'I'm always uncomfortable when I see pre-school boys in soft-play areas with tons of gel making their hair stick up. They look like proper little shit heads and I know it's that kind of boy who will get my three-year-old daughter pregnant when she becomes a teenager.' (*Not jumping to conclusions at all!*)

 'Never dress your kids in matching outfits unless you want them to look like a right bunch of tosspots, like the Osmonds.' (*I had no idea that flared white jumpsuits were still in fashion.*)

 'I have four boys and I really, really hate mothers of girls. Yes, those annoying women who throw me pitiful looks of patronizing smugness as they sit there with their perfectly behaved and zen-like daughters, dressed in beautiful chocolate-brown-and-pink funky little dresses, tights and oh-so-cute matching shoes. And there's me – desperately trying to keep control of my shouty, snotty three-year-old, who keeps yelling "poo head" at the top of his voice, and holding a baby who looks like he rolled round in a charity-shop bin and came out wearing some 1980s Thomas the Tank Engine woollen jumper (which was new on that morning, actually) because clothes manufacturing for boys hasn't quite taken on the cuteness of girls' clothes yet. Arggggh!' (*Methinks the lady doth require counselling.*)

 'You can't buy decent footwear with shoelaces for kids these days. All the reputable shoe shops only seem to sell shoes that fasten up with velcro. So we are raising a generation of children who can't tie shoelaces. It's pathetic. I don't want my little boy to grow up to be a useless lump who only wears slip-on shoes because he doesn't know how to tie his laces. Kids these days know nothing about survival. Most of them will never learn to tie a reef knot. Or a simple figure-of-eight knot. Or a Full Windsor knot in their tie. Or a proper bow tie. We will be a nation of elastic-bow-tie-wearers. It makes me livid.' (*I never realized that the interweaving of two pieces of thread could evoke such outrage.*)

'Rainbow tie-dye on children is so awful. And it's especially bad if worn with leggings. It's fine for grown-ups to look like woolly, tree-hugging hippies if that's what they want, but to inflict it on your own children is just unkind.'

(*I suppose the seventies Billy Connolly look can't be carried off by many people.*)

♀ 'To me, dressing a toddler in a leather biker's jacket is a cardinal sin. At my son's playgroup there is a little boy whose mother dresses him in a black leather jacket, jeans and white T-shirt. His mum thinks he looks like the Fonz, but he doesn't. He looks like a tiny dickhead.' (*Now that's no way to speak about a child, is it?*)

♀ 'Dungarees on children over the age of eighteen months should be banned. It looks weird and creepy. And you just know that mothers of children who wear dungarees are the kind of women who wear pinnies in the kitchen and only have sex on Wednesday nights. Boys in dungarees look all sinister, like Damien from *The Omen*, and girls look all homely and square, like Isla St Clair. And if they need a wee, they can't get undressed quickly enough, so kids in dungarees always wet themselves. Which isn't very fair. In fact it's a form of child abuse.' (*Isla St Clair?*

Quick, get Social Services round to all dungaree-wearing children NOW.)

 'It makes me sick when I see little girls dressed like prostitutes. Little cropped tops showing off their midriffs, tiny little miniskirts, and don't get me started on the make-up issue. My four-year-old daughter was recently given a pair of knickers with the slogan "Mini Minx". It's a total outrage. It makes me so angry and sick. Why can't our little girls just run around barefoot in floaty white gowns that come down to their ankles?' (*Angry Victorian dad has spoken.*)

 'I hate novelty babygros. Anything that has ears or a tail. Dressing your baby as a teddy bear or a pussycat really annoys me. I know newborn babies are like pets – cuddle them, feed them and get nothing in return – but there's no need to reinforce it, for crying out loud.' (*That's right. If you want a fluffy animal, go and buy a guinea pig. Their poos are much easier to clean up.*)

15. LANGUAGE

Inflicting the Language of the Gutter on Your Kids

Warning: if you don't like swearing then avert your eyes right now, because this section contains fucking loads of it. You see, you're not allowed to swear when you have kids. Thou shalt not say shit, fuck, cunt, bollocks, wanker or bugger in front of your kids. It's fucking difficult. More so than, say, giving up smoking or alcohol during pregnancy. In those cases, although it's tough you get to think about your actions and ultimately you have control over your own success or failure. With swearing, it's a reflex action. You stub your toe – your immediate reaction is to shout 'Shit!' a good second before the 'pain' message sent by your toe has actually reached your brain. Some stupid idiot pulls out suddenly in front of your car – you impulsively shout 'Fuckwit!' at the top of your voice, even before you slam on the brakes. Swearing is as involuntary as breathing, which is why so many parents do it in front of their kids.

Kids love to learn new words and then test them out to see how they sound. Kids are like sponges – they soak up words and then repeat them parrot-style because it makes them feel grown up. Most of the time they haven't got a clue what a word means, which can lead to embarrassing and awkward moments for parents.

Real Parents' Top Five Inappropriate Uses of Swear Words by Kids

* Loudly in the middle of Sainsbury's: '*Have we run out of fucking toilet paper, Mummy?*'
* Pointing at the next-door neighbour: '*Is that the thieving bastard, Daddy?*'
* Announced to everyone in the waiting room of a quiet doctors' surgery: '*My name is Katie and I'm in a shitty mood!*'
* Daddy and son are standing in a queue at the post office. Son turns to the lady behind and says, '*Hello. My daddy's bollocks are really sore today. Shall we put some cream on them?*'

> * In a quiet bit at the Christmas Nativity play. **'Does Jesus have an arsehole, mummy?'**

So you see, it's never good to let children hear you swear. But what is the alternative? Well, there are three options:

> * Quit swearing. But that would be like asking someone to stop blinking. It ain't gonna happen.
> * When an incident occurs that necessitates a swear word, go to another room or perhaps the garden shed, and scream blue murder at a safe distance from innocent ears. But this requires considerable self-control and isn't practical if you are, say, driving a car.
> * Replace your swear words with substitutes.

Now clearly, unless you are one of those weird people who never utters a rude word, the third option is the only way forward. But it's more difficult than it seems. First of all, you have to think of an alternative word that carries the same weight, impact and satisfaction as a swear word. Will 'fiddlesticks' or 'sugar' really suffice when your little angel has just whacked you hard between the legs with his plastic pirate sword? I don't think so, and not only that, but you'll sound like some dreadful jolly-hockey-sticks Enid Blyton character. So you need a substitute word that sounds as good as a swear word. I've asked some parents to share their alternative expletives; here are the best:

Real Parents' Top Ten Satisfying Replacement Swear Words

* **Cock-a-doodle-doo.** (*This is the most popular replacement swear word. It's easy to remember, satisfying to say and totally non-offensive.*)
* **Clackers.** (*As in 'Oh Clackers!'*)
* **Poopcakes.** (*As in 'What a pile of poopcakes.' Perhaps a little bit twee, but could be used in any situation.*)

* **Quim.** (*Yes, it might be just a tad pretentious, but the mummy who uses this is an English teacher.*)
* **Twunt.** (*Amalgam of 'twat' and 'cunt' – but try saying 'twuntface' out loud. It's actually ruder than any real swear word, so think hard before using it in front of the kids. Do you really want them calling their friends a 'twunt'?*)
* **Plaps.** (*Contraction of 'piss-flaps'. I've tried using this one myself and it's rather good.*)
* **Wibbly wang.** (*As in 'What a load of wibbly wang.'*)
* **Fufflenuff.** (*A slightly rubbish 'fuck' replacement, but bonus points for creativity.*)
* **Shakin' Stevens.** (*As in 'Oh Shakin' Stevens'. A surprisingly enjoyable alternative to 'shit'.*)
* **Blurglegunt.** (*Drifting towards Vogan poetry here, but a good word nevertheless.*)

So now you are newly armed with harmless profanities. The difficult part is remembering to use them. I suppose it's rather like learning a new language – a huge effort on your part. But always remember, effort = extra parenting brownie points.

16. SEX

What Time Is Love?

We all know that people go a bit weird when it comes to sex during pregnancy. Some women become raging nymphomaniacs, whilst others would rather eat their own hair than have sex when pregnant. Some men are terrified to have sex with their pregnant partner, scared that the baby somehow 'knows' that sex is taking place or that they might hurt or knock the baby. Others find women with enormous baby-filled bellies incredibly sexy and take great pleasure in doing the deed. But whatever the case, there is no denying that once the sperm has done its spermy job, sex is never the same again.

Parents are constantly moaning that they have no time for themselves, let alone time for an intimate relationship. But while most of us will readily admit that our kids have changed our sex lives and we perhaps aren't as frisky as we used to be, our libidos are still going strong. Sort of. But trying to fit a bit of sex into our busy schedules isn't as simple it seems. So what is the best time of the day for parents of pre-schoolers to have it off?

Morning Glory

If, like me, you have kids who wake every day at stupid o'clock on the dot, a morning shag is the last thing on your mind and would be pretty much impossible. Having a toddler jump up and down on your head with an enormous, soggy nappy slapping your ears isn't ideal, and even if you do somehow manage to distract your child with the TV in your bedroom, the sound of Mr Tumble singing enthusiastically about froggies plopping in the pond is a bit of a passion killer.

Afternoon Delight

Some parents manage to do it when their child has an afternoon nap. Are they mad? Your house looks like an explosion in Toys R Us, your kitchen is an environmental health hazard, there are

bottles to sterilize, soiled clothes to wash, carpets to vacuum, emails to reply to, phone calls to return, dinners to prepare, floors to wash, toilets to clean, and all you can think about is having shenanigans? Shame on you.

Evening Shuffle

So you've bathed the kids, read them a story and they are sound asleep. It's seven thirty – the night is young. You sit down for your meal, crack open a bottle of wine and talk about your day.

'I had a shit day at work. I'm exhausted.'

'Really? That's too bad. I've had a crap day too. The car broke down in the Blackwall Tunnel, causing a three-mile tailback, Emily pooed herself by the cheese counter in Sainsbury's and Oliver ate half a tin of cat food and threw up all over the baby.'

'Great. Shall we have sex?'

'Fuck off.'

Not Tonight, Josephine

Even if you manage to find a time slot in your

day for sex, the chances are that whilst one of you will be up for a bit of action, the other won't be. When you are lying in bed, utterly exhausted to the core, with the theme tune to *Space Pirates* going round and round in your head, the last thing you need is your other half trying to get all fruity with you. So if you want to get out of your marital duties, here are some of the finest excuses as used by real parents:

Real Daddies' Top Five Excuses for Not Having Sex

* 'I can't stop thinking about the poor starving children in Africa.'
* 'My penis is broken.'
* 'I accidentally watched a documentary on Channel 4 about dwarves with elephantitis and it's put me right off.'
* 'I want to make another baby.'
* 'I was in the mood half an hour ago, but you took so long to come to bed that now all I can think about is whether or not Macca Pacca suffers from OCD.'

Real Mummies' Top Five Excuses for Not Having Sex

* ✱ 'I might be sick.'
* ✱ 'I might wee myself.'
* ✱ 'You've ruined me.'
* ✱ 'There's no point, because you go completely numb down there after you've had a baby.'
* ✱ 'It's not worth it. After three kids it'd be like waving a Biro in the Channel Tunnel.'

Giving Head?

Something very odd happened to me one evening recently. Odd and slightly embarrassing. Oscar had come home from nursery infested with headlice once again. So we all had to go through the process of rubbing headlice lotion into our hair. We did the kids first, put them to bed, and after Jim had applied the lotion to his own head it was my turn. Now my hair is quite long, so I needed a bit of help. Jim sat himself down on the sofa, whilst I sat on the floor between his legs to watch *EastEnders* on the telly. I'm not entirely sure whether it was the glass of Sauvignon Blanc

I was drinking, or the fact that I was lusting over one of the actors in *EastEnders* (NOT Ian Beale, by the way), but as Jim rubbed the Hedrin into my hair I started to feel a bit peculiar. Oh my God! I had become sexually aroused by the application of stinky, greasy nit lotion to my head. I was officially a pervert. Of course, I didn't actually tell Jim that he had just introduced me to a weird new fetish, as he would probably have been delighted and I was far too knackered to be getting down to any funny business. So I just carried on watching *EastEnders* and pretended that it hadn't happened.

I must stress that I am not alone with my inappropriate turn-on. A mummy friend recently admitted to me that she almost became a woman possessed when she watched her husband making a papier mâché present for their son. 'He was sat at the kitchen table on a summer's evening, bare-chested, with his hands all covered in paper and glue, carefully sculpting Humpty Dumpty. The Humpty was really rubbish and looked like it had been made by a three-year-old, but my husband looked so sexy. He looked just like Patrick Swayze in *Ghost*. I was tempted to go and entwine my fingers in his mucky hands like Demi Moore, but the thought of cleaning up all that glue put me right off so I put the kettle on instead.'

17. WIND

Top Trumps

The humble fart. We all do them. Obviously, some more than others. But nobody farts more than kids. From the moment we welcome our babies into the world we marvel at their botty burps.

'Wow, that was a big one. Clever girl!'

'Aaah look, she's smiling. Oh no, it was just a blow-off.'

'Is that a poo or a fart? Uh-oh, it's a poo.'

At some point in their lives, children begin to find farting funny. And what's not to laugh about? Farts make a funny noise, they come out of your bottom and sometimes they smell really, really bad. But the funniest thing about 'letting one go' is the different euphemisms that parents use for it.

Real Parents' Farting Euphemisms

- **Toot.** *(Brings a whole new meaning to Dick Van Dyke singing 'Toot Sweets' in Chitty Chitty Bang Bang.)*
- **Cuckoo.** *(I kind of like the idea of a little bird popping out of a bottom to say hello.)*
- **Trump.** *(A bit of a classic, this one. Has stood the test of time well.)*
- **Woofty.** *(I can't help feeling that this one is a bit politically incorrect.)*
- **Poot.** *(I would imagine that a small creature like a vole might 'poot'.)*
- **Grumble.** *(Who wants a whingey arse?)*
- **Snap, Crackle and Pop.** *(Whichever way you look at it, bottoms and Rice Krispies just don't go together.)*
- **Fluff.** *(Bum fluff?)*
- **Nobin.** *(I Googled 'nobin', just in case it is a real word, and apparently it is. A nobin is an organic molecule used for asymmetric catalysis, which I'm guessing is a fart.)*
- **Squidge.** *(Yuck.)*
- **Hufty.** *(The thought of a shaven-headed*

lesbian jumping out from between two
buttocks is a bit weird, really.)

* **Tweet.** (Aaah! If only a blow-off really did
sound like birdsong. The sweet tweets from
under the duvet in the morning.)
* **Roar.** (Obviously a powerful and majestic
noise from your pants.)
* **Bing Bong.** (You can get farting ringtones
for your phone. I'm sure you can get farting
doorbells too.)
* **Gobble.** (Oh, this one is horribly wrong, isn't
it?)

I was going to end this subject here, because I think you
have to deal with enough bum stuff on a day-to-day basis
as a parent without my wittering on about flatulence.
However, some of the parents who so openly shared
their fart euphemisms with us also revealed their own
more adult dysphemisms. Now I have to say that I was
quite surprised! In my house, a blow-off is a blow-off for
everyone who does them, but I thought you might like to
learn some of the secret names that parents use when the
kids aren't around. Warning: these are utterly repulsive!

Real Parents' Disgusting Fart Terms

* Shit snore.
* Trouser cough.
* Arse parcel.
* Rectal honk.
* Beefer.
* Rip snorter.
* Egberter.
* Grandpa. (No, I have no idea either!)
* Turd honk.
* Shit fumes.

Man alive! If these words are from the mouths of responsible parents, there is no hope for the next generation.

18. YUMMY MUMMIES

Why Do We Hate Them?

What can I say about Yummy Mummies that hasn't already been said? They are the ultimate symbol of modern-day motherhood: beautiful, stylish, elegant women who wear their immaculately attired children as fashion accessories. You can't open a magazine without the likes of Victoria Beckham, Kate Moss, Angelina Jolie and Gwen bloody Stefani showing you how easy and glamorous it is to be a mum. Of course, it's a completely unrealistic phenomenon co-created by celebrities and the media, but it has shaped today's social attitudes to parenthood. Aside from parenting books, nothing sets new mothers up for a feeling of inadequacy and failure like the Yummy Mummy concept.

I wanted to be a Yummy Mummy, and thought that my job as a BBC breakfast radio presenter might perhaps help me achieve my goal. I had the same boss as Jonathan Ross, Chris Evans, Dermot O'Leary, Lauren Lavern and Claudia Winkleman, so I hoped that a little bit of showbiz glamour might rub off on me. Sadly, it didn't – I was prone to turning up to work at five a.m. exhausted and ratty, with aching, leaky boobs, dressed in my revolting, milk-stained pyjama top, with unbrushed hair that made me look like a Chuckle Brother.

I had to face the hard fact that I was unable to be a sexy, desirable mother in a showbiz setting. But the svelte figure of the wealthy A-list Yummy Mummy is everywhere – she's on the front cover of glossy magazines, on television adverts, on billboard posters and in high-street shop windows, causing regular mums to spew up vast fountains of jealousy.

Real Mummies' Top Ten Most Annoying Celebrity Yummy Mummies

★ **Tess Daley.** 'Nothing has ever annoyed me more than the sight of her prancing round the garden in a bikini just ten weeks after giving birth to her second child. She looked amazing. Her stomach as flat as an ironing board and her knockers all pert and marvellous. I've had two kids and if I jumped around in the garden in a bikini my unrestrained excess loose flesh would probably knock me unconscious.'

* **Victoria Beckham.** 'I want to like her, I really do, but she's always got a face like a smacked bum. I mean, come on girl, cheer up – three gorgeous sons, the world's sexiest man in your bed, more money than you'll ever need, beautiful designer clothes and shoes given to you for free – why the fuck have you got such a cob on? Come and live with my husband and I'll show you real misery.'

* **Davina McCall.** 'She's always harping on about her perfect natural home births and how great and easy breastfeeding was and how she still has great sex with her husband, blah blah. I had three stressful labours, my tits are now hanging by my thighs, my fanny is like the Grand Canyon and my husband

laughs when he sees me naked. Davina, you can take your great sex life and fuck off.'

* *Angelina Jolie.* 'I seriously worry about her. I think she might have an addictive personality or something. I mean, how many children do you need, for God's sake? I think she may need therapy for child addiction. I'd be terrified if I saw her near any of my kids – she might take a fancy to my youngest, 'cause he's well cute, and he might end up in the back of her car when I wasn't looking. Do they have child-addiction therapists in LA?'

* *Gwen Stefani.* 'Have you seen how skinny her arms are? She's the same age as me, with as many kids, but her arms are like sticks whilst mine are like wobbly nanna flaps.'

* *Kirstie Allsopp.* 'Her first baby was enormous, weighing over eleven pounds, and she had a C-section. My first baby also weighed over eleven pounds but he was delivered naturally. My poor, poor fanny is still recovering three years later. If I could go back in time, I would beg for a Caesarean. It's not hate I feel, it's just jealousy. But

intense jealousy. If you could only see my fanny you'd understand.'

✱ **Madonna.** 'No one looks less like a mother than Madonna. She looks as if she spends all day in the gym or having her hair and make-up done. I'd just love to see her face smeared with Marmite. I think then I might like her.'

✱ **Nigella Lawson.** 'She always makes batches of food to freeze for her kids so they can have healthy and wholesome snacks after school. How does she find the time to be so perfect? Who cleans up all the cooking mess? How is she then able to look all sexy and delicious? How does she make her kids eat her healthy food? Why does *my* daughter only want to eat biscuits, ice cream and crisps? I'm sorry, Nigella, but you piss me right off.'

✱ **Gwyneth Paltrow.** 'Oh, she's into all that organic vegetarian malarkey, isn't she? That Coldplay husband of hers really needs to put his foot down. All that flaky healthy green seaweed stuff isn't good for his children. I hope he regularly pops to Asda to stock up on black pudding and pork pies. Kids need

protein and energy. Vegetarians don't eat
enough pork pies and the kids will suffer.'

★ **Katie Holmes**. 'Her ridiculously cute kid
and her film-star husband really wind me
up. Families that good-looking shouldn't be
allowed to parade their beauty in public. It's
obnoxious.'

Parental Advisory Warning: The Yummy Mummy Hate Campaign

But there is another type of mother who is even more
annoying than the A-list Yummy Mummy. The non-
celebrity Yummy Mummy. You can spot them a mile away:
trim, expensively dressed, pushing super-groovy buggies,
sipping on lattes and laughing in the sunshine without a
care in the world.

When Oscar was younger, I used to take him regularly to
a music group. There was one woman who always caught
my attention and stood out from the other mummies in the
group. She looked fantastic, her hair was well groomed,
her face was fully made up, her nails were perfectly
manicured and her casual clothes were all designer labels.

She looked as if she was ready for a big Saturday night out. I couldn't figure out how on earth she looked so incredible at nine thirty a.m. when the rest of us all looked as though we'd spent the night sleeping in a bush. And then I found out from another mummy that she was a Premiership footballer's wife. Ah! Now I understand. You see, the world of the Yummy Mummy is very different from our world. It's a world without poo in your hair or crusty snail trails of snot all over your cardigan. It's a world of money, nannies and, most importantly, time. And that's possibly the most irritating thing about Yummy Mummies – that they actually have time to do things other than do battle with children. They have time to brush their hair. Time to go shopping for nice clothes. They have all the time in the world. And their designer-label kids, like pretty much everything else in their lives, have simply become a rather grotesque way of displaying their wealth and perfection.

Real Mummies' Top Five Fantasy Yummy Mummy Mishaps

★ 'Nothing angers me more than Yummy Mummies walking three abreast, hogging the pavement with their enormous three-wheeled pushchairs. I like to imagine a posh, horsy, tummy-tucked mummy called Imogen trying to set up her massive Bugaboo stroller. She gets in a bit of a pickle and her pashmina shawl gets caught up in the stroller. She's trapped and can't free herself and starts to panic, but the more she struggles, the more she gets drawn into the complex mechanics of the pushchair. Eventually she disappears completely into the jaws of the stupidly oversized buggy and dies of starvation. Thinking about this makes me happy.'

✱ 'Wouldn't it be great if all the rich Yummy Mummies hanging out in a trendy coffee shop in Primrose Hill were horrifically burned when the coffee machine exploded and sprayed them with boiling-hot cappuccinos. Actually, no, I've changed my mind; let's make them all drown in a giant vat of their own toddlers' snot. Ha ha!'

✱ 'I like the idea of a really ditzy Yummy Mummy falling out of her 4×4 army tank and running over herself in a Brian Harvey from

East 17 kind of way. He really was a stupid prick, wasn't he?'

* 'How about if the overworked, underpaid, stressed-out nanny gets asked to do one task too many and it tips her over the edge. She becomes really bitter and devises a cunning plan where she seduces the husband and makes him dress up in a PVC gimp suit with just a hole for his willy to poke through. Then she films them doing the dirty deed and posts the yucky DVD to the Yummy Mummy wife, who is so repulsed that she throws herself off the roof of her house.'

* 'I have a fantasy scenario where an elegant Yummy Mummy (who doesn't look unlike Kate Moss) is at the top of her townhouse staircase. She slips on a Thomas the Tank Engine the maid has failed to tidy up and falls dramatically down the stairs, landing face-down on her Jimmy Choo stilettos which her four-year-son Tarquin has been trying on and has inconveniently left lying upside-down. The £500 four-and-a-half-inch

> heels go through her eyeballs and into her
> brain, killing her instantly. Did I go into too
> much detail?'

So there you have it! A candid and slightly alarming insight into the screwed-up minds of parents, and proof that the media creation of the Yummy Mummy can stir up powerful emotions. Yikes!

19. POLITICAL CORRECTNESS

Foot-in-Mouth Disease

One of the most wonderful things about pre-school children is their innocence. They are completely unaffected and have no preconceptions or prejudices. Since children don't know the rules of polite conversation, they frequently push the boundaries of good taste. Taboos and political correctness don't even exist for them. It's all very cute and lovely – until they suddenly utter something in public so inappropriate that you don't know whether to laugh, cry or pray that the ground will open up and swallow you whole.

Real Parents' Top Five Embarrassing and Politically Incorrect Public Outbursts by Their Kids

 'I was at the supermarket with my three-year-old son, when a severely disabled woman in a wheelchair joined the queue behind us. I immediately foresaw an awkward situation and tried desperately to distract my son so that he didn't notice her. But the queue was moving so slowly that he got bored and started wandering about. And then he saw her. He looked her up and down before coming over to me and saying loudly, "Daddy, that lady in the pushchair with the silly face is so lazy." I nearly died.'

 'I took my son to McDonald's for the first time as a special treat. I really wish I hadn't bothered. As we walked up to the counter, my son took one look at the poor guy taking our order and said, "Wow! That man is the fattest man I've ever seen. Is he the fattest man in the world, Daddy?"'

'My four-year-old daughter and I were shopping in the supermarket and I stopped to put some tampons into the trolley. My daughter obviously saw this as a perfect opportunity to show off the new information that she had learned when she had recently seen me change my tampon. She turned to the poor gentleman next to us, who was looking at the toothpaste, and very precisely said, "My mummy puts tampons into her vagina to stop it bleeding." The man walked away sharpish.'

 'I took my six-month-old daughter to be weighed at the baby clinic, and as it was his day off nursery, my four-year-old son came along too. Just as I was putting my daughter on the scales, my son said very seriously to the health visitor, "My mummy drinks loads of wine to take away the pain of motherhood." I'm teetotal so I have no idea where he had heard that phrase, but I was convinced that Social Services would turn up on my doorstep at any moment.'

'I was in my local newsagent's with my little girl. As I was getting the money out of my purse to pay Mr Patel, my daughter very loudly and clearly said, "Mummy, you don't like black babies, do you?" She was actually referring to the Jelly Babies that I was buying at the time, but I was absolutely mortified.'

There are some moments when an innocent comment from a child can really highlight what a paranoid, uptight world we live in. I had taken Oscar for a wee in the ladies' toilets at our local arts and culture centre. The toilets were pretty busy and we squeezed into a cubicle so that Oscar could do what he had to do. As he lifted the toilet seat and aimed into the bowl he loudly asked me, 'Mummy, do you love my penis?'

Yeah, not really the kind of question I wanted to be asked within earshot of a roomful of strangers. I could hear little sniggers coming from some of the other cubicles, so I ignored Oscar, which prompted him to ask me the same question again and again until I was forced to say, 'Yes, I love your penis.'

I thought that this would be the end of the conversation, but I was wrong.

'Does Daddy love my penis?'

Cue more giggling from the other cubicles.

'Yes, he does.'

'Does Grandad love my penis?'

'Yes.'

'Does Grandma love my penis?'

'Yes. Hurry up and do a wee, please.'

'Does Wilfie love my penis?'

'Yes, he does. Now please do your wee.'

And it was at this exact moment that a woman from the cubicle next to us shouted, 'And I love your penis too!'

'And so do I!' said a voice from another cubicle.

'Me too!' said another.

Oscar was absolutely delighted and the wee finally came out. Hurrah!

20. THINGS THAT MAKE YOU GO 'BLEURGH'

It's a fact – children are revolting. They do disgusting things that would make you retch if it weren't for your parental cast-iron stomach. Yes, parents have an extraordinary ability to deal calmly with the yuckiest situations. When you're a parent, you can watch a child puke up jelly and ice cream all over the table at a birthday party and just carry on munching your slice of cake without even flinching. You are tough enough to join the SAS. That's how tough you are.

When I was a little girl, I had a friend who had her very own bogey collection. She used to carefully pick them out of her nose and stick them on the edge of her bedside table. Then she would lie down and admire her rather large collection before she went to sleep. She was dead proud of her bogeys. Of course, this was utterly disgusting, but at the time I didn't think anything of it. In fact, I was actually quite tempted to begin a collection of my own. I didn't, though, as any little greeny that I pulled from my nose would always end up straight in my mouth rather than on a wall display. Oh come on, be honest – you know you used to sneak a tasty snotty snack when you thought no one was looking!

Real Parents' Top Ten Revolting Things Done by Their Children

 'My four-year-old and his friend from nursery were playing in the garden when I noticed they were doing something a bit odd. From a distance it looked as if they were biting each other's hands, so I went over to see what they were up to. It turned out that they were cleaning each other's nails with their teeth, nibbling out all the dirt and eating it.'
(*Yes, it's gross, but at least they weren't cleaning their toe nails.*)

'My two-year-old started licking worms whenever she found one. I thought this was bad enough, but soon she got even more curious and started to bite them in half. Then of course the inevitable happened – she ate one, and now worm eating is one of her favourite things to do in the garden.' (*A lot of people don't realize that worms are highly addictive. It begins with licking, moves on to biting, then eating, and then before you know where you are you are injecting them two or three times a day. Be warned.*)

 'One of the most vile things I have ever witnessed was my little boy and his playmate picking bogeys and putting them in each other's mouth. It makes me feel a bit sick just thinking about it.' (*Now that really is love. I definitely don't love my children enough to eat their bogeys.*)

 'My three-year-old son once stood up in the bath and aimed his penis at his eighteen-month-old sister, who was quite happily splashing about next to him. An enormous jet of wee shot up into the air and my little girl attempted to catch it in her mouth. Thank God he missed.' (*On special occasions the Manneken Pis statue in Brussels is attached to a keg of beer. The little boy statue pisses out booze from his winkie, which is caught in cups and given to passers-by. Was this a copycat incident?*)

 'Once when we were on holiday, my thirteen-month-old son came up to me with a black stone he had picked up. I just sort of looked at it and threw it aside. I then bent down to pick him up and noticed he had this black stuff on his teeth, and upon closer inspection it became apparent that it was not a stone he had given me, but actually cat shit which he had clearly been nibbling. And it wasn't just any cat shit. It was foreign cat shit.' (*That foreign cat shit doesn't taste anywhere near as good as British cat shit. Not as meaty.*)

 'My two-year-old daughter threw up on the

kitchen floor after jumping around a bit too vigorously. Our cat couldn't get to the sick fast enough and immediately started eating it. I turned my back for two seconds to grab a towel and when I turned around, my daughter was on her hands and knees with the cat, eating her own vomit. I have never seen anything so disgusting in my life.' (*But at least she was sharing. Always look for the positive.*)

 'I was in a café one afternoon and my one-year-old son was playing on the floor beside me. There was an old man sitting at the next table eating a massive piece of coffee cake. He had caught my eye earlier because he was making revolting slurping noises as he drank his tea from his saucer. In fact he was grossing me out a bit, but at the same time I couldn't stop staring at him. He took a big bite of his cake, had a little chew and then started hacking up a big chesty cough. Everything suddenly went into slow motion as I watched a piece of chewed-up cake fly out of his mouth and land on the floor right in front of my son. I tried to grab him but I was too late. He picked up the gobbed-out cake and shoved it in his mouth. It was a hideous moment that will stay with me for ever.' (*Spittle-enriched cake is apparently incredibly high in immunity-boosting nutrients.*)

 'I found my three-year-old son sitting on the floor next to the dog bowl with a knife and fork, happily eating the dog food. What really annoyed me was that he was usually such a picky eater and would refuse point blank to use cutlery. Yet there he was, carefully using his fork to place dog food in his mouth with a look of sheer bliss, as though he was eating the finest delicacy in the world. I hate kids sometimes.' (*Stick that in your toddler recipe book, Annabel Karmel.*)

 'My four-year-old son kindly took his bowl over to his very short-sighted grandma on Christmas Day to offer her a chocolate. She took one, ate it, then commented on how tasty it was and took another. In fact she pretty much polished off the whole bowl. It was only when I had a look at the last few chocolates that I realized my son had been feeding her guinea-pig poos. Needless to say, I didn't tell the mother-in-law.' (*Guinea-pig poos actually taste similar to wild truffles. Fact.*)

 'I once found my two-year-old daughter on her knees, kissing our pet Labrador's bumhole. I screamed in horror and pulled her away immediately. When I asked her why she had been doing it she explained that the dog's bottom looked sore and so she was kissing it better.' (*How kind and thoughtful.*)

Pukey Parents

It's pretty much a foregone conclusion that kids do exceptionally unpleasant things. But what about us parents? Let's be honest – there are certain things that we do on a day-to-day basis that are socially unacceptable. It's time to face facts, folks: we are as revolting as our children.

Disgusting Things Parents Do

* *Putting your child's feet in your mouth.* Your three-year-old has been running around in trainers all day and her little feet stink to high heaven. But you just can't resist the urge to pop those whiffy feet in your mouth, can you? OK, so you made those beautiful feet and they're cute and tiny and perfect. But try to remember how utterly revolting it looks to everybody else as you gorge on those Gorgonzola tootsies.

* *Inspecting poo.* Whether it's bottom wiping or nappy changing, all parents carefully examine their children's poo. We just like to know that everything is OK in that department. 'Oooh look, there's a piece of sweetcorn and that's a bit of sausage. Oh, and there's that hairclip I was searching for.' It's like a lucky dip. You never know what you'll find.

* *Eating food that your child has dropped on the floor.* You would never normally do this, would you? Perhaps it's because you are constantly telling your child not to waste food or maybe it's because

you are simply mental. I don't know, but I've done it myself. Your child drops a biscuit on the café floor. You pick it up, but don't return it to your child because it's dirty. So you shove it in your mouth instead. What are you – a human dustbin or something?

* **Tissue substitutes.** When your child's face is dripping with fresh snot and you can't find a tissue anywhere, you will use anything instead. And I mean *anything*. A teddy bear, a pair of pants or a sock from the washing basket, your scarf, your finger, the cat, oven gloves, your knee, even your own hair. Parents can be very resourceful, especially if a pair of slimy, sticky, snotty, puckered lips are coming your way for a kiss. It's amazing how quickly you can find a tissue substitute then.

* **Spitting on a tissue and wiping your child's face.** You used to hate it so much when your mum or granny gobbed on a hanky and then spread it all over your face. You swore that you would never ever do it to your own child. But then you notice your child has a blob of Marmite on her chin and before you know what's going on, you've

spat and wiped. It's a reflex action. But it's still disgusting.

* **Eating what your child has spat out.** Your eighteen-month-old son has taken a bite of his cheese sandwich and had a little chew before deciding that he doesn't like it. So he spits it back on to his plate. And what do you do? You gobble it up, of course. Yummy.

* **Biting your child's fingernail off.** Once when I was having lunch with a friend, Oscar came up to show me his fingernail, which was partly hanging off. I simply put his finger in my mouth and bit off the nail so that it didn't get caught on anything. I put the nail in the bin and Oscar happily went back to his playing. Job done. I turned back to my friend, who looked utterly appalled. She thought it was one of the most revolting things she had ever seen. She doesn't have kids, so I just told her to fuck off.

* **Leaving the house with filthy clothes.** Your T-shirt is covered in yoghurt, milk and porridge, and a teeny-weeny but deadly smelly fleck of poo is smeared on

your jeans, yet you haven't got time to change your clothes before you leave the house. If you are heading off to meet fellow parents then there isn't a problem. If you are going anywhere else, consider yourself a social outcast. You look and smell really bad.

* **Cleaning your baby's dummy with your mouth.** You are pushing your toddler round the children's farm and she drops her dummy right next to a cowpat. Stupidly it's the only dummy you have brought out with you and your daughter is now screaming her head off. What do you do? Isn't it obvious? You pick up the dummy and stick it in your mouth, hoping that your super spit will disinfect the animal poo, E. coli, rabies, ringworm and foot and mouth disease that it may now carry. Then you put the dummy back in your toddler's mouth.

* **Discussing bodily functions in public places.** As soon as you have children, you forget that it isn't very polite to talk about bodily functions around other people. You are in a quiet café when you say loudly, 'What's that smell?'

'I've just done a blow-off, Daddy.'

'Christ, that's a bad one. Do you need a poo poo?'

'No.'

'Are you sure?'

'Yes, Daddy.'

'Do you need a wee wee?'

'No.'

'Then why are you holding on to your penis?'

'I think I need a poo poo and a wee wee, Daddy.'

'OK, come on then. Let's hope it's a better poo than the one you did this morning.'

'That was a yucky poo, Daddy. It went everywhere.'

'Yes, it did.'

And you wonder why the couple on the next table have left half their chocolate cake and are giving you filthy looks.

WE LOVE THEM REALLY!

Parenting is a work in progress and no matter how many manuals and handbooks we consult, we can never be fully prepared for just how much of an impact pre-school children make on our lives. From the instant they decide to enter the world, they immediately strip away our dignity when they make us squeeze out a poo in the delivery room in front of a midwife and four student doctors. New mums and dads should use this moment as a benchmark for the years ahead, as it only gets worse. From stuffing cold cabbage leaves down your nursing bra to ease the pain of mastitis, to losing your Tena Lady incontinence pad out of your trouser leg at yoga class, it's safe to say that your life definitely isn't the same as before.

So after all our moaning and complaining about how undignified, difficult and revolting parenting actually is, you wonder why on earth we bother in the first place. The answer is always the same for all mums and dads, but makes absolutely no sense at all. Parenthood is simply fucking brilliant! Go work that one out!